ASIAN DEVELOPMENT BANK KNOWLEDGE MANAGEMENT ACTION PLAN 2021–2025

KNOWLEDGE FOR A PROSPEROUS, INCLUSIVE, RESILIENT, AND SUSTAINABLE ASIA AND THE PACIFIC

MARCH 2021

ASIAN DEVELOPMENT BANK

ADB

Notes:
In this publication, "$" refers to United States dollars.

Cover design by Keisuke Taketani.

CONTENTS

FIGURES AND BOXES

ABBREVIATIONS

ADB	–	Asian Development Bank
COVID-19	–	coronavirus disease
DEfR	–	development effectiveness review
DMC	–	developing member country
SDCC-KC	–	Knowledge Advisory Services Center
KMAP	–	knowledge management action plan
WPBF	–	work program and budget framework

EXECUTIVE SUMMARY

The Knowledge Management Action Plan (KMAP) 2021–2025 connects the reforms of the Asian Development Bank (ADB) to improve how knowledge is managed across all its business processes. The KMAP supports Strategy 2030 by strengthening ADB's ability to better deliver tailored knowledge solutions, together with financing, to developing member countries (DMCs). The KMAP emphasizes increasing collaboration, improving the quality and efficiency of knowledge services, making knowledge work more attractive, and using a country-focused approach to benefit DMCs. The KMAP will increase ADB's value addition, boost client satisfaction, and bolster ADB's role as a trusted knowledge provider.

Building on previous action plans, ongoing initiatives, and recommendations of the Independent Evaluation Department's *Knowledge Solutions for Development: An Evaluation of ADB's Readiness for Strategy 2030*, the KMAP aims to achieve the following:

(i) Move from counting knowledge products and services to providing knowledge solutions that clients need.
(ii) Reduce knowledge silos, connect people, and increase collaboration.
(iii) Increase the relevance and quality of knowledge.
(iv) Strengthen the capacity of country teams, including resident missions, to manage knowledge and strengthen relationships.
(v) Optimize the contribution and learning of staff members, consultants, and partners to benefit the bank.

The KMAP leverages ongoing ADB initiatives and reforms, including the implementation of the action plan of the review of ADB's resident mission operations, the culture transformation initiative, the country partnership strategy reform review, the review of technical assistance operations, the digital agenda, the innovation framework, and others. The KMAP follows five principles that will guide departments and teams in tailoring their knowledge management road maps:

(i) **Differentiated.** Knowledge services across DMCs meet different needs.
(ii) **Balanced.** Demand and supply–driven, top-down and bottom-up knowledge services advance sustainable development in DMCs.
(iii) **Culture and learning driven.** The importance of organizational culture and learning is recognized by all of ADB and reflected in all its processes and systems.
(iv) **Technology enabled.** ADB leverages information technology and uses it well.
(v) **Results focused.** The results of knowledge work are monitored and measured.

The KMAP is supported by a Theory of Change that identifies 3 outputs and 10 key actions:

(i)   People and culture improved to incentivize, create, and promote knowledge solutions.
  (a) Align the KMAP with initiatives to transform ADB's culture.
  (b) Recruit, develop, foster, and incentivize staff members who have the needed knowledge management competencies.
  (c) Implement the innovation framework.

(ii)   Processes and systems upgraded to encourage client-oriented knowledge creation, flow, and use.
  (a) Strengthen country knowledge programming.
  (b) Create a connected enterprise knowledge network.
  (c) Strengthen and clarify measures to guide teams in developing quality knowledge products.

(iii) Relationships built and nurtured across departments in ADB and with knowledge partners in DMCs and beyond for better-connected knowledge networks.
  (a) Create a culture of collaboration through strategic and efficient knowledge partnerships.
  (b) Strengthen the resident missions' role in advancing relationships.
  (c) Reinforce relationships between different ADB functions and foster a "One ADB" approach.
  (d) Cultivate relationships with international financial institutions and other intergovernmental organizations on knowledge management.

As the KMAP has implications for everyone in the organization, all departments and offices will be responsible for its implementation, and the expanded knowledge management group for its coordination. The Knowledge Advisory Services Center under the Sustainable Development and Climate Change Department will serve as the secretariat to expedite the KMAP's implementation.

I. WHY A KNOWLEDGE MANAGEMENT ACTION PLAN?

A. Strategy 2030 and Knowledge Management

The Knowledge Management Action Plan (KMAP) 2021–2025 connects bank-wide reforms to improve how ADB manages knowledge in all its business processes to give effect to the knowledge provisions of the Asian Development Bank (ADB) Strategy 2030 (Box 1). Strategy 2030 is clear about how ADB should strengthen its knowledge services:

(i) Increase collaboration by instituting a "One ADB" approach, bringing together knowledge and expertise from across the organization to increase learning, innovation, and impact in developing member countries (DMCs).

(ii) Improve the quality of knowledge services through deeper analysis and research, expedite greater knowledge sharing across countries, and make business processes more efficient.

(iii) Use country-focused approaches, emphasizing practical knowledge that fits local conditions; identify lessons; and replicate good practices across the region and beyond.

Box 1: Strategy 2030—the Asian Development Bank's Compass for Change

Despite the devastation caused by the coronavirus disease (COVID-19) in 2020, the dramatic changes that have swept Asia and the Pacific since the establishment of the Asian Development Bank (ADB) are indelible. Middle-income developing member countries (DMCs) now outnumber low-income ones. In 2002, more than 1 billion people (or over a third of the region's population) were extremely poor. In 2008, those numbers fell to 758 million or a little over a fifth. In 2015, they plunged to 264 million or less than a tenth.[a] Still, much more needs to be done, particularly in response to the COVID-19 pandemic. Hundreds of millions remain poor, climate change and disasters threaten swathes of the region and even entire countries, food insecurity stalks millions, and many cities need to drastically improve living conditions. Women have made greater economic, political, and social strides than ever, yet they are still hobbled in ways that men are not.

Knowledge, innovation, and partnerships will sharpen ADB's efforts to work with DMCs to meet these challenges and achieve the four core targets of Strategy 2030: accelerate progress in gender equality, climate operations, private sector operations, and long-term cofinancing. While ADB continues to finance solutions and catalyze finance for DMCs, it will increase the value of its operations by creating and sharing knowledge to advance economic resilience and sustainability.

The following are Strategy 2030's knowledge goals that inform the KMAP:

(i)   Strengthen ADB as a proactive knowledge provider.
(ii)   Fortify institutional capacity in DMCs.
(iii)   Pilot test and scale innovative approaches and solutions.
(iv)   Expand knowledge partnerships.
(v)   Consolidate explicit knowledge and disseminate it through diverse channels and digital technologies.
(vi)   Improve the flow and capture of relevant tacit knowledge.
(vii)   Give staff members incentives to conduct knowledge work and promote knowledge across ADB, with sector and thematic groups leading the efforts.

Other knowledge provisions in Strategy 2030 include

(i)   encouraging knowledge sharing among upper-middle-income DMCs;
(ii)   supporting public and private sector operations and providing advisory services and knowledge support;
(iii)   boosting knowledge sharing and collaboration between subregions; and
(iv)   mobilizing financial resources for ADB trust funds and deploying them efficiently for capacity development, project preparation, and knowledge work.

[a] ADB. 2018. *Asian Development Outlook 2018 Update: Maintaining Stability amid Heightened Uncertainty.* Manila.

Source: ADB. 2018. *Strategy 2030: Achieving a Prosperous, Inclusive, Resilient, and Sustainable Asia and the Pacific.* Manila.

B.   ADB as a Knowledge Organization in Strategy 2030

Under Strategy 2030, ADB provides a spectrum of finance and knowledge services and partnerships, depending on the country context, the size of ADB operations in the country, and the complexity of its portfolio. Knowledge management is key to understanding where ADB can add the most value in a DMC to help achieve the Sustainable Development Goals. To stay relevant as a leading and trusted knowledge provider in Asia and the Pacific, ADB must integrate its knowledge work across sectors and themes and the public and private sectors, ease cross-disciplinary problem-solving, and advance innovation. A single expertise, sector, or theme is no longer adequate to provide effective knowledge solutions to development challenges. ADB must understand complex systems and learn from regional and global best practices while tailoring them to countries' needs. Once the regional "family doctor," ADB must now become the regional "advisor" that supports DMCs with bespoke solutions on their long-term sustainable development paths.[1]

In its new role, ADB must not only supply predictable long-term financing and mobilize financial resources for development and innovation but also provide high-quality policy advice and institutional and capacity development (Box 2).[2] The combination of finance, advice, and training will help DMCs decide (i) what kind of development projects and programs are most relevant, (ii) how they will be financed and designed, (iii) how they fit into a country partnership strategy and a national development plan, and (iv) who needs to be involved in the work.

Box 2: Gender Equity in Development—Asia Women Leaders Program

Started in 2014 as an Asian Development Bank signature initiative, the Asia Women Leaders Program bridges significant gaps in women's leadership capacity. The program targets senior women government officials in finance, planning, and infrastructure ministries who can influence their countries' policies. The program strengthens officials' knowledge, skills, networks, and confidence. Women leaders motivate and mentor participants, sharing their experiences and insights, and top-level trainers teach techniques to improve communication, negotiation, and alliance building. The program has trained more than a hundred middle-management leaders and has been rolled out in several countries in collaboration with national gender agencies and civil service academies. The program imparts leadership skills to the alumni network virtually during the pandemic until in-person training can resume.

Source: Asian Development Bank.

Achieving the desired future requires transitions (i) from ADB as a knowledge bank (focusing on "know *what*") to a solution bank (focusing on "know *how*"), (ii) from a focus on the number of knowledge products and services produced per department to measurement of the impact of knowledge solutions applied to complex problems across DMCs, (iii) from collection and capture of knowledge to co-creation and curating of knowledge solutions across ADB with partners and

---

[1]   ADB. 2017. *ADB through the Decades: ADB's First Decade (1966–1976)*. Manila.
[2]   Middle- and upper-middle-income countries may request complex knowledge solutions and policy advice, while low-income and fragile and conflict-affected countries may require more institutional and capacity development. However, some middle-income countries continue to seek support for institutional development and some fragile and conflict-affected countries benefit from policy advice.

innovation through iterative processes, and (iv) from knowledge trapped in silos and repositories to knowledge solutions flowing through networks. These transitions go hand in hand with ADB's progress toward optimizing efficiency, quality, and value addition. Processes must be continuously improved through quantitative and qualitative feedback and piloting and modeling of new ideas and technologies.[3]

ADB cannot rely on incremental change to transform the way it conducts business. The Independent Evaluation Department's 2020 report on ADB's knowledge solutions challenges the very assumption of incremental change.[4] DMCs face a world vastly different than that of 1966, when ADB was established. ADB must substantially strengthen its ability to deliver tailored knowledge solutions in addition to finance, invest in staff learning, bolster country teams' ability to lead policy dialogue, transform ADB's culture, and reform systems and human resource management. Such changes mean not only focusing on improving existing processes and increasing efficiency but also creating greater value for clients.

C.   The COVID-19 Pandemic: From Crisis to Opportunity

The KMAP draws on ADB's coronavirus disease (COVID-19) response, which showcases how ADB can respond to crises by leveraging collaboration, digitalization, and agility (Box 3). Lessons learned include the following:

(i)   **Digitalization.** Staff members managed business processes virtually and digitally. Teams in different time zones quickly embraced digital collaboration tools.

(ii) **Collaboration.** The pressure to deliver made staff members practical, more collaborative, open-minded, and ultimately effective.

(iii) **Agility and responsiveness.** COVID-19 highlighted how connected development challenges are and how ADB needs to align bank-wide initiatives and mobilize and expedite expertise across sectors and themes.

(iv) **Management.** Management style became more inclusive, team-driven, inquisitive, and open to risk.

(v)   **Culture change.** Hierarchies were flattened, meetings became more inclusive, and expertise was sourced from across the bank. Staff members worked in large teams to directly apply their tacit knowledge to project design and policy dialogue with DMCs.

(vi) **Remaining challenges.** It was difficult to locate needed expertise across the bank, foster debate and discourse, and create space for collaboration beyond working on ADB documents. Management relied on the personal dedication of staff members, who were themselves affected by the crisis and delivered above and beyond their regular annual workplan. Such extraordinary efforts are not sustainable in the long run. Managers must consider how to balance workloads and cultivate a culture of collaboration.

---

[3]   K. Dalkir. 2011. *Knowledge Management in Theory and Practice.* Second edition. Cambridge, MA: MIT Press.
[4]   ADB. 2020. *Knowledge Solutions for Development: An Evaluation of ADB's Readiness for Strategy 2030.* Manila.

Box 3: How the COVID-19 Pandemic Transformed the Asian Development Bank

The coronavirus disease (COVID-19) pandemic is a threat to Asian Development Bank (ADB) member countries, staff, and operations. Within days, ADB had to move its entire business processes to the virtual space, manage teams across continents and time zones, funnel tacit knowledge across sectors and themes into projects and programs, and deliver services rapidly to clients. The crisis increased the sharing and capture of tacit knowledge in blogs, webinars, and meetings.

In 2020, besides quickly providing a large resource envelope via the Comprehensive Response to COVID-19,[a] ADB released more than 1,000 COVID-19–related knowledge products and services and knowledge dissemination support in various formats: blogs, awareness-raising materials, webinar series such as the Policy Actions for COVID-19 Economic Recovery Dialogues, Asia Impact, the Insight ADB series, videos, and other multimedia formats supported policy dialogues and knowledge sharing on how to manage the crisis. A key message was that mitigating the crisis requires greater (i) regional cooperation; (ii) social safety nets, transfer programs, and gender equity; and (iii) fiscal stimulus and green infrastructure investment, including through public–private partnerships.

Teams need to continue collaborating—with each other internally and with external partners—on assessments, analyses, and problem solving. The COVID-19 pandemic is not the result of a virus alone. It is the consequence of well-known deficiencies across multiple systems and issues, including health and gender. The crisis highlighted the need for a moral framework for development and knowledge work: what investments, policies, and plans to prioritize; who should benefit; who pays; and what the intergenerational impact is of each intervention. Understanding these relationships and complexities requires leadership, values, foresight, mindfulness, experience, and technical skills. ADB's knowledge workers of tomorrow apply more than theoretical and analytical knowledge. They solve complex problems in creative and innovative ways to improve lives in Asia and the Pacific.

[a] In March 2020, ADB announced a $6.5 billion initial package to tackle the immediate needs of its developing member countries. ADB. 2020. *ADB's Comprehensive Response to the COVID-19 Pandemic.* Manila. See also COVID-19 (Coronavirus): ADB's Response.

Sources: ADB website; ADB blogs; and ADB. 2020. *Navigating COVID-19 in Asia and the Pacific.* Manila.

II. KNOWLEDGE GAP ANALYSIS

A. Organizational Constraints on Strengthening Knowledge

While ADB has made great strides in embracing advancements in knowledge management, analyses carried out over the years have documented constraints and gaps in ADB's knowledge work and culture of knowledge sharing and collaboration across the bank and with DMCs.[5] A shortcoming of past knowledge management initiatives is that good practices have not been highlighted or shared sufficiently so that they become the standard. ADB needs to move to the next phase of maturity, which involves, among other things, better ADB-wide knowledge sharing and organizational learning. ADB still faces the following challenges:

(i) **Cultural gaps.** ADB's organizational culture generally does not value knowledge work as much as lending, leading to a great deal of, but not always strategic and high-quality, knowledge work. Small technical assistance projects, which can greatly influence policy, are valued less than large loans in staff performance reviews and career progression. ADB's culture does not sufficiently nurture discussion, debate, and dialogue, and does not enable fast learning from failures and successes across teams.

(ii) **Structural gaps.** Organizational silos and competing resource envelopes inhibit effective and purpose-driven coordination of lending and knowledge work to meet Strategy 2030's objectives. The structural separation of knowledge-intensive, administrative, and operations departments creates an artificial rift between operations and knowledge work.

---

[5] The more prominent analyses highlighting the constraints include (i) ADB. 2012. *Special Evaluation Study on Knowledge Products and Services: Building a Stronger Knowledge Institution.* Manila; (ii) ADB. 2013. *Knowledge Management Directions and Action Plan (2013–2015): Supporting "Finance++" at the Asian Development Bank.* Manila; (iii) ADB. 2020. *Knowledge Solutions for Development: An Evaluation of ADB's Readiness for Strategy 2030.* IED Thematic Evaluation Study. Manila; (iv) ADB. 2017. *Lessons from Country Partnership Evaluation: A Retrospective.* Manila; (v) ADB. 2017. *Knowledge, Finance, and the Quality of Growth: An Evaluative Perspective on Strategy 2030.* Manila; (vi) ADB. 2014. *Corporate Evaluation Study: Role of Technical Assistance in ADB Operations.* Manila; and (vii) ADB. 2020. *Review of ADB's Resident Mission Operations.* Manila. Discussions that have increased the understanding of constraints—and ways to overcome them—include the Board Management retreat of 2018, the Office of the Vice-President for Knowledge Management and Sustainable Development retreats of 2018–2020, the 2018 Knowledge Forum, and the informal Board seminar of September 2020 and the deep-dive session with the Board in October 2020 on the proposed KMAP. Finally, the Roundtable Discussion on Knowledge Management for Development in early December 2020, which brought together leading academicians and practitioners (including from the private sector), yielded valuable insights on the state of play in knowledge management governance and management, in theory and in practice.

    (iii) **Institutional and/or procedural gaps.** ADB builds on decades of knowledge management frameworks and has demonstrated effective knowledge management in theory and practice.[6] ADB has dedicated knowledge management functions but still needs to tackle the following:

        (a) lack of clear incentive structures for knowledge work;

        (b) more reliance on lending and transactions in DMC portfolios and less on knowledge;

        (c) scarce resources for knowledge work in middle-income countries;

        (d) limited long-term capacity development and institution building in low-income countries and fragile and conflict-affected situations;

        (e) excessive outsourcing of knowledge work (largely through overreliance on consultants);

        (f) lack of rigorous peer review of knowledge work;

        (g) varying levels and quality of knowledge management tool applications;[7]

        (h) uneven resident mission capacity to inform and manage knowledge work;

        (i) a static country knowledge plan exercise that does not dynamically respond to the changing needs of DMCs; and

        (j) weak knowledge-coding measures in repositories, databases, and client management registries, which have not maximized knowledge work across the bank or enabled strong and effective knowledge partnerships.

    (iv) **Lack of focus on results.** ADB has not sufficiently emphasized reporting on and measuring knowledge solutions and their impact in DMCs.

    (v) **Lack of maturity in data management.** ADB still relies on huge manual efforts to access, validate, and reconcile data to support operations and respond to requests within ADB and from partners and clients. Data integration and data management must be automated and upgraded.

B.   Theory of Change

At the core of the KMAP is a Theory of Change that explains how to bridge knowledge management gaps so that ADB can become a leading and trusted provider of knowledge solutions, and contribute to better-informed policies, innovative programs and projects, and operations in DMCs (Figure 1).[8] The KMAP's Theory of Change identifies the following assumption and expected result: DMCs have to ensure that their development includes low-carbon growth, climate resilience, environmental consciousness, human capital development, gender equity, and socioeconomic recovery from the COVID-19 pandemic. Knowledge solutions and lessons from other countries and from decades of project implementation are needed to achieve the triple bottom line of developing human capital, mitigating climate change, and advancing sustainable economic development. The Theory of Change includes three pillars or outputs:

    (i) **People and culture incentivized to create and promote knowledge solutions.** To build a culture of collaboration, allowing the free flow of ideas and appreciating staff members as knowledge workers, ADB (a) implements a values-based culture transformation initiative aligned with knowledge management; (b) recruits staff members with the

---

[6]   O. Serrat. 2010. *Knowledge Solutions: Tools, Methods, and Approaches to Drive Development Forward and Enhance Its Effects.* Manila: ADB; O. Serrat. 2008. Notions of Knowledge Management. *Knowledge Solutions.* 18. Manila: ADB; and O. Serrat. 2017. *Knowledge Solutions: Tools, Methods, and Approaches to Drive Organizational Performance.* ADB and Springer.

[7]   See Appendix 3 for examples of knowledge management tools.

[8]   Drawn from ISO 30401 (Knowledge Management Systems—Requirements), particularly on knowledge management enablers (human capital, processes, technology and infrastructure, governance, and knowledge management culture).

knowledge management competencies for their jobs and improves talent management and staff learning; and (c) puts in place an innovation framework to enable staff members to learn from "what works and what does not" and to test new ideas.[9]

(ii) **Processes and systems streamlined for client-oriented knowledge creation, flow, and use.** To deepen the understanding of clients' knowledge needs, provide channels that allow agile collaboration, and strengthen measures to deliver quality knowledge solutions, ADB (a) strengthens country knowledge programming; (b) establishes a closely connected enterprise knowledge network where information on sector and thematic work and new initiatives, among others, can be accessed and augmented; and (c) produces relevant and quality knowledge products and services that result in effective knowledge solutions.

(iii) **Relationships built and nurtured across departments within ADB and with knowledge partners in developing member countries and beyond.** To encourage sharing, piloting, and scaling up of innovative ideas, ADB (a) leverages stronger and more strategic knowledge partnerships to deliver knowledge solutions to clients; (b) updates the capacity of resident mission teams and their leadership to ensure solutions are provided for delivering the best results with available resources; (c) institutes the "One ADB" approach by clarifying and confirming the roles of all team members (e.g., country directors and resident missions, sector directors and divisions, sector and thematic groups, the Economic Research and Regional Cooperation Department, among others) in client relationships; and (d) nurtures relationships with international financial institutions and other intergovernmental organizations on knowledge management.

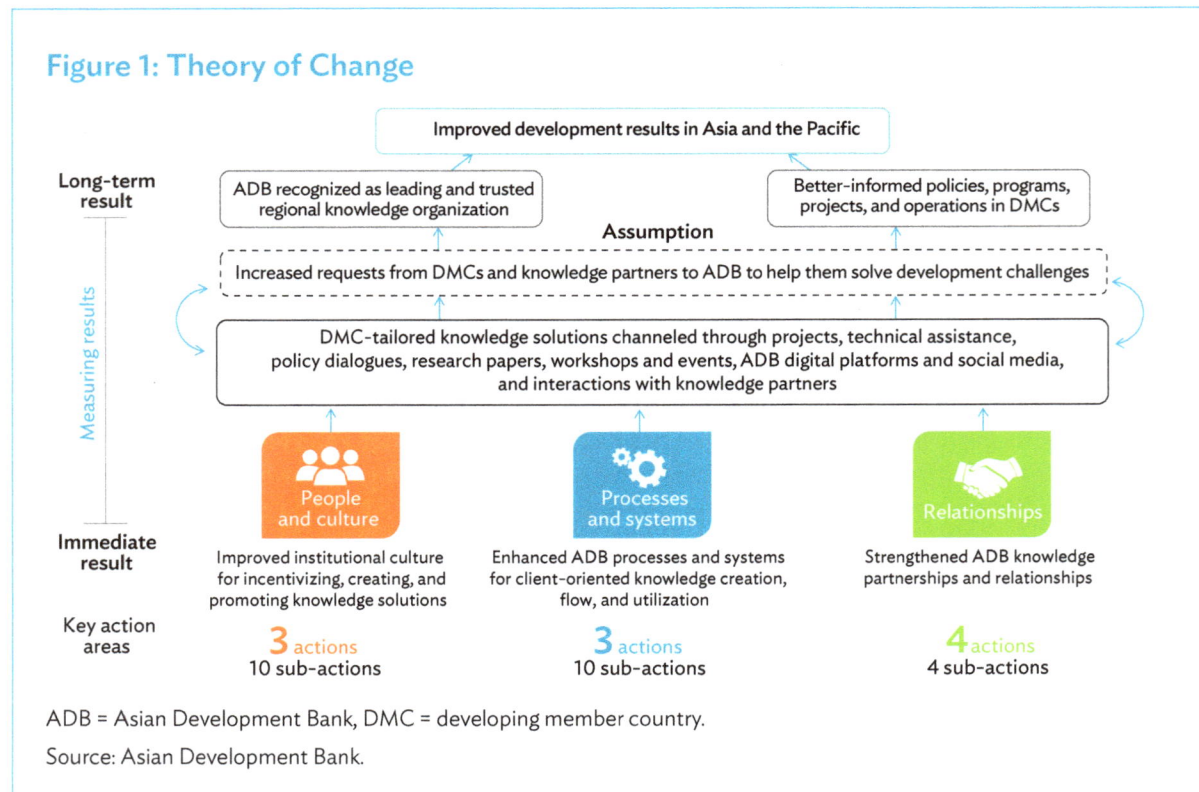

Figure 1: Theory of Change

ADB = Asian Development Bank, DMC = developing member country.

Source: Asian Development Bank.

---

[9] The proposed ADB innovation framework strengthens the drivers of innovation and advances ADB's ability to identify, support, test, and scale innovation. The 2020 Innovation Fair showcased innovative knowledge solutions and approaches. ADB. 2020. *Faces of Innovation*. Manila.

ADB and DMCs will increasingly tailor knowledge solutions through policy dialogue, research work, projects, technical assistance support, knowledge events, ADB digital platforms and social media, and interactions with knowledge partners. By doing so, DMCs and knowledge partners will increasingly request ADB to help solve their development challenges.

C.   Tackling the Constraints on Effective Knowledge Management

ADB must achieve the following to move from counting knowledge products and services to providing knowledge solutions that clients need:[10]

(i)   **Related to people and culture.** Optimize the contribution and learning of staff members, consultants, and partners to benefit the bank. ADB must consider how it should develop the capacity of staff members, create a culture that values knowledge management and lifelong learning, and ensure that staff members are incentivized and recognized regionally and globally as experts. ADB should expedite the exchange of knowledge among not only staff members but also consultants; build an expertise locator, with staff member and consultant profiles; forge partnerships with clear outcomes; and borrow knowledge judiciously from think tanks and universities.

(ii)   **Related to processes and systems.**
  (a)   Increase the relevance and quality of knowledge in the knowledge management cycle (Appendix 1). ADB is good at capturing and, to some extent, storing knowledge in reports. However, it must improve how knowledge is reused and how quality is ensured, and pay more attention to knowledge dissemination, application, and transfer and to learning in the context of country portfolios. ADB must integrate knowledge activities into lending and across silos and recognize everyone in ADB as a knowledge worker.
  (b)   Strengthen country teams and build resident missions' knowledge management capacity. ADB should improve upstream analysis and assessment and better coordinate country diagnostic work within ADB and with country partners.[11]

(iii)   **Related to relationships.** Break down knowledge silos to connect people and increase collaboration. Knowledge is not created in a vacuum but through partnerships and networks, both internal and external. ADB must stress knowledge and functions, not hierarchies or silos; ease and foster knowledge collaboration between knowledge and operations departments; and encourage interconnected, self-organized communities and sharing of knowledge between internal groups, including the ADB Institute, and external resources and partners.

---

[10]   Knowledge management means generating, capturing, and disseminating knowledge; applying lessons learned (e.g., opening new business lines based on what has been learned); and engaging externally, collaborating extensively, and upscaling learning.

[11]   ADB is improving, on a pilot basis, its country knowledge programming as part of the country partnership strategy in the Philippines and has incorporated lessons learned into the KMAP. The lessons include the need to focus the country knowledge programming exercise on (i) identifying a DMC's knowledge needs and gaps, (ii) discussing which knowledge gaps ADB can help fill and what kind of knowledge services it can offer, (iii) emphasizing a "One ADB" approach to promoting knowledge, (iv) preparing a knowledge dissemination plan, and (v) synchronizing the work of the 3-year rolling country operations business plan with a similar period for knowledge products and services.

These issues point to the need for a KMAP that (i) is based on principles and is forward-looking, (ii) serves as a platform to build synergies for parallel reform efforts,[12] and (iii) guides action to achieve Strategy 2030's objectives. Reflecting the strategy's priorities, the KMAP will build on, expand, and reinforce existing good practices, and apply lessons learned on how knowledge management tools are used to drive climate operations (Box 4), expand private sector engagement (Box 5), and mobilize long-term cofinancing with knowledge (Box 6). All these areas are among the key priorities of Strategy 2030.

Box 4: Knowledge to Drive Climate Operations—Indonesia

In their nationally determined contributions (NDCs), countries have outlined their commitments to achieving the goals of the Paris Agreement, including greenhouse gas reduction targets and actions for adaptation. However, current collective commitments are insufficient to meet the Paris Agreement's goal of limiting global temperature rise to well below 2 degrees Celsius. All countries need to exert substantial and long-term efforts to raise their NDCs. To support its developing member countries (DMCs), Asian Development Bank (ADB) established NDC Advance, a technical assistance platform that helps them mobilize finance and build capacity to achieve their NDCs. Using the platform, DMCs can translate their NDCs into climate investment plans and identify priority climate projects; access innovative financing; and develop methods and tools to measure, monitor, and report on NDC commitments. NDC Advance is part of Supporting the Implementation of ADB's Climate Change Operational Framework 2017–2030. ADB is active in the NDC Partnership, working closely with other development partners.

In 2020, NDC Advance financed a consultant posted to ADB's Indonesia Resident Mission to help integrate climate and disaster considerations into the country partnership strategy, 2020–2024, and identify potential investments aligned with Indonesia's NDC. NDC Advance support deepened the country team's understanding of how to tackle climate change, build climate and disaster resilience, and increase environmental sustainability as provided in Strategy 2030. The support was instrumental to developing the country partnership strategy to strengthen resilience, focusing on climate change and the environment. The assistance enabled on-demand expertise to expedite engaging with the government and development partners. Indonesia's experience shows that providing targeted in-country support can lead to more ambitious climate operations in country partnership strategies.

Source: Asian Development Bank.

---

[12] Many innovation reforms and initiatives are ongoing in ADB and intricately linked with the knowledge agenda. They can be viewed from the perspective of the KMAP's three pillars: (i) people and culture: a culture transformation initiative, revamped leadership programs, a talent management program, the establishment of the innovation framework, and a better-targeted learning strategy; (ii) processes and systems: the review of technical assistance operations, the execution of the digital agenda (including digitalization of sovereign operations and the digital workplace), the review of the country partnership strategy reform, and the review of ADB's resident mission operations and the related action plan; and (iii) relationships: the review of ADB's approach to knowledge partnerships and the framework for better engagement with upper-middle-income countries.

Box 5: Knowledge to Expand Private Sector Operations—Georgia

Until 2017, the Asian Development Bank (ADB) nonsovereign portfolio and pipeline in Georgia was limited. Private sector players had little awareness of ADB and limited access to private sector experts from ADB headquarters. As a result, ADB faced competition from other development finance institutions. ADB sovereign and nonsovereign operations had not yet been integrated.

ADB posted an expert to the Georgia Resident Mission to help the country team deepen its understanding of national relationships and dynamics, strengthen relationships with clients, and create new networks with partners. Collaboration became more seamless because of team interactions, resulting in faster identification of nonsovereign opportunities and creation of joint projects and initiatives between sovereign and nonsovereign operations. The joint gender mainstreaming workshop series, for example, which has held three in-person and online sessions since 2019, helped ADB raise awareness of and interest in the bank's growing focus on gender-related projects. The series strengthened the network of nonsovereign clients and positioned the bank as a "finance + knowledge provider" that promotes gender balance and diversity in the C-suite.

Supported by strategic knowledge work, ADB's nonsovereign portfolio has consolidated through innovative and landmark transactions, including (i) the first green bond from Georgia and the South Caucasus, (ii) the first Private Sector Operations Department health-care project in Central and West Asia, (iii) technical assistance to explore the potential of geothermal resources in the country, and (iv) loans to financial institutions that support small and medium-sized enterprises.

Source: Asian Development Bank.

Box 6: Knowledge to Mobilize Cofinancing for Community Resilience—Southeast Asia

Scaling up community investments in resilience to climate and disaster risk was a priority of the Integrated Disaster Risk Management Fund, administered by the Asian Development Bank (ADB) and financed by the Government of Canada.[a] Taking a multipronged approach, the fund supported national governments, such as that of Myanmar, where the Myanmar National Framework for Community Disaster Resilience identified opportunities to intensify investments through poverty reduction policies and programs.[b] The multi-stakeholder framework anchored the ADB-financed Resilient Community Development Project, approved in 2019.[c]

Recognizing that investments need to be driven by communities in partnership with local governments, the fund supported four pilots in Indonesia, the Philippines, and Viet Nam. Three of the pilots were implemented by grassroots women's organizations and captured the tacit knowledge of local communities on strengthening resilience. More importantly, the pilots allowed ADB to partner with the Huairou Commission, a global coalition of grassroots women's organizations working in 45 countries.[d] The fourth pilot worked with a microfinance institution to study the feasibility of a disaster-resilient microfinance product, which could be scaled up by ADB investments.[e]

continued on next page

Box 6 continued

The lessons learned from the pilots were documented and shared with stakeholders, including developing member country agencies and donors.[f] Knowledge from the pilots was captured in technical guidelines on boosting resilience through social protection programs,[g] community-driven development programs,[h] and women-focused investments,[i] thereby strengthening ADB's climate actions in social development and gender projects.

The knowledge work recognized the importance of ADB engaging in emerging global topics such as the devolution of climate finance to build local resilience, which led to ADB working closely with the International Institute for Environment and Development, a leading global climate resilience think tank.[j] The community resilience–related outputs of the Integrated Disaster Risk Management Fund demonstrated the vast need to help countries in Asia and the Pacific escalate community resilience investments. The coronavirus disease pandemic has highlighted why countries are vulnerable and why local resilience must be reinforced.

[a] ADB. *Integrated Disaster Risk Management Fund.* Manila.
[b] PreventionWeb. *Myanmar National Framework for Community Disaster Resilience: Promoting People-centered, Inclusive, and Sustainable Local Development.*
[c] ADB. *Myanmar: Resilient Community Development Project.* Manila.
[d] Huairou Commission. *Grassroots Women at the Frontline of COVID19.*
[e] ADB. 2016. *Disaster-Resilient Microfinance: Learning from Communities Affected by Typhoon Haiyan.* Manila.
[f] ADB. 2017. *Accelerating Sustainable Development: Investing in Community-led Strategies for Climate and Disaster Resilience.* Manila.
[g] ADB. 2018. *Strengthening Resilience through Social Protection Programs: Guidance Note.* Manila.
[h] ADB. 2018. *Scaling Up Resilience-Building Measures through Community-Driven Development Projects: Guidance Note.* Manila.
[i] ADB. 2020. *Enhancing Women-Focused Investments in Climate and Disaster Resilience.* Manila.
[j] International Institute for Environment and Development.

Source: Asian Development Bank.

III. KNOWLEDGE MANAGEMENT ACTION PLAN 2021–2025

A. Principles-Based Approach

The KMAP is based on the following principles:

(i) **Differentiated.** Knowledge services across DMCs consider different needs.
(ii) **Balanced.** Demand and supply–driven, top-down and bottom-up knowledge services are balanced.
(iii) **Culture and learning driven.** The KMAP recognizes the importance of organizational culture and learning.
(iv) **Technology enabled.** Information technology is used efficiently.[13]
(v) **Results focused.** The results of knowledge work are measured (Appendix 2).

The KMAP needs to take an iterative approach. The KMAP follows the latest knowledge management research and recommendations, which suggest that knowledge management is improved not by one big action or a silver bullet but by many small actions, usually staff behavior, which need to be nudged. Often, the sharing of good practices creates experiences that change behavior. The benefits from these many small actions materialize over time and not overnight.

B. Building on Experiences

The KMAP builds on nearly 2 decades of concerted knowledge management efforts in ADB.[14] The plan focuses on measurable indicators (drawing from the Corporate Results Framework) for key results of a robust Theory of Change and incorporates Strategy 2030's differentiated

---

[13] The digital agenda's program on the digital workplace and connected data aims to establish data management standards and processes. Along with platforms to support a centralized database, the digital agenda supports improved searchability of corporate documents and records, enabled by the electronic document and records management system. The system will provide records management features in SharePoint, easing the governance and retention of valuable corporate records amid an increasing volume of documents (nearly 10 million as of 2021) and promoting the use of a corporate metadata scheme to improve information retrieval.

[14] Previous knowledge management action plans were (i) the 2004 Knowledge Management Framework, which focused on improving knowledge management systems and databases (ADB. 2004. *Knowledge Management in ADB*. Manila); (ii) the Knowledge Management Action Plan 2009–2011, which reinforced communities of practice and coordination between knowledge and operations departments (ADB. 2009. *Enhancing Knowledge Management under Strategy 2020: Plan of Action 2009–2011*. Manila); and (iii) the Knowledge Management Action Plan 2013–2015, which guided ADB's Strategy 2020 in, among others, establishing the operations cycle in DMCs as the basis for planning and applying knowledge solutions, and fostering a culture of sharing knowledge (ADB. 2013. *Knowledge Management Directions and Action Plan (2013–2015): Supporting "Finance ++" at the Asian Development Bank*. Manila). The action plans responded to the needs of their time, and as the world changed, knowledge management adapted.

approach to engage with different DMCs in ways that meet their specific knowledge needs and increase the focus on knowledge solutions (Appendix 3).[15]

Lessons from preparing earlier KMAPs and the analysis of ADB's myriad processes for operations and back-office support point to the need for a stronger bank-wide harmonized approach to managing knowledge.[16] As knowledge transcends the work of every staff member, the KMAP cannot be prepared in isolation and should be synchronized with efforts directed at people, processes, technology, and relationships—the key assets that define knowledge-driven organizations and increase organizational maturity.[17]

The KMAP benefits from the latest research on good knowledge management practices and principles gleaned not only from the literature but also from global best practices (Box 7).

Box 7: Good Knowledge Management Practices and Principles

(i) Knowledge is intangible and complex; it is created by people and resides with people.

(ii) The untapped potential of knowledge must be harnessed to deepen the value of services to developing member countries.

(iii) The focus of knowledge management must be sharpened to clarify organizational objectives, strategies, and needs.

(iv) Agile knowledge management practices must be adopted that are customized and context specific; no single knowledge management solution fits all organizations.

(v) Knowledge management needs to enable shared understanding and requires interaction between people and empathy for their viewpoints, using content, processes, and technologies (Appendix 4 provides an overview of knowledge tools).

(vi) Knowledge is not managed directly. By managing the working environment, one nurtures the knowledge lifecycle.

(vii) Culture is critical for effective knowledge management.

(viii) Knowledge management should be iterative, incorporating learning and feedback cycles, and support innovation.

Note: Knowledge management practices and principles that merit consideration can be seen in the knowledge management initiatives of other multilateral development banks and development partners, including (i) the African Development Bank's Knowledge Management Strategy, 2015–2020; (ii) the World Bank's Knowledge Management Action Plan, 2017–2020; and (iii) the International Fund for Agricultural Development's Knowledge Management Framework, 2019–2025. The Roundtable Discussion on Knowledge Management for Development, held on 1 December 2020, brought together experts from academia and the private sector to share experiences and research. The experts confirmed that the Knowledge Management Action Plan is a comprehensive approach cognizant of the latest research.

Sources: ARK Group. 2019. *A Guide to Global Best Practice and Standards in KM*; ISO 30401:2018(en) Knowledge Management Systems—Requirements; APQC. 2012. *Knowledge Management at Arup Group Limited: Case Study*; and C. Collison, P. Corney, and P. Lee Eng. 2019. *The KM Cookbook: Stories and Strategies for Organizations Exploring Knowledge Management Standard ISO 30401*. London: Facet Publishing.

---

[15] ADB. 2019. Measuring, Reporting and Recognizing Knowledge Products and Services and Knowledge Solutions. Memorandum. 19 October (internal). Addendum. Each department submits knowledge solutions, which are evaluated using defined criteria before being presented at the annual operations review meeting. The initiative was the first ADB-wide exercise to measure and report how ADB knowledge helped solve DMCs' development problems.

[16] A substantive range of analytical work feeds into the KMAP. The drafters relied, among others, on the review of various initiatives ongoing at ADB (for example, resident mission operations, the innovation framework, the country partnership strategy, and technical assistance) and of actions implemented under KMAP, 2012–2015. See footnote 5 for citations of other relevant analytical work.

[17] K. Dalkir. 2005. *Knowledge Management in Theory and Practice*. Burlington, MA: Elsevier.

C.   Proposed Actions in the Knowledge Management Action Plan

The KMAP brings synergies across bank initiatives and reforms and focuses on culture change, more responsive client services, and better use of networks (Appendix 5). The three pillars include specific corporate activities, which need to be tailored to each department.

Pillar 1: Invest in people and culture. The actions supporting this pillar are aligned with ADB's values-based culture transformation initiative program and build on the review of ADB's culture. ADB's core values will anchor the KMAP and various bank-wide culture change initiatives to embrace collaboration and knowledge promotion, among others. Culture change will help promote the understanding that each staff member is a knowledge worker.

ADB needs to recruit staff members with the relevant knowledge management competencies for their jobs. ADB's competency framework must include knowledge management competencies and behaviors. Recruitment and performance review should strengthen the assessment of knowledge management capabilities, including collaboration, agility, and a desire for lifelong learning.

A knowledge culture is supported by excellent talent management and staff learning, which require a corporate learning platform and a principles-based learning strategy so that staff members can access all types of relevant learning programs easily and monitor their impact on performance and staff development. Staff learning will improve with the development of curated learning programs and well-managed on-the-job learning for specific job families and functions (for example, for country directors), including digital skills, and for managers to better support staff members' efforts to develop and promote lifelong learning. Equally important is the improvement of an expertise locator to easily identify expertise, networks, and communities across the bank.

An important part of culture change is embracing a common understanding of innovation, fostering a less risk-averse approach to doing things, and learning from mistakes.[18] The KMAP will link with the ADB innovation framework and support its implementation.[19]

Pillar 2: Improve processes and systems. Actions supporting this pillar will promote Strategy 2030's country-differentiated approach and strengthen ADB's capacity to deliver tailored knowledge solutions to clients. Providing knowledge products and services to and with clients requires deep understanding of countries' knowledge needs and capacity, and the mapping of collaboration opportunities to create, apply, and transfer knowledge.

Better processes are needed to strengthen country knowledge programming. Resident missions are ADB's primary channels for engaging with DMCs, and country programming is the main interface for engagement. ADB needs to refine the country knowledge programming process (Box 8) and strengthen all country teams[20] by training staff members and/or repurposing vacant

---

[18]   Greater innovation and efficiency are demonstrable results of good knowledge management practices.

[19]   The draft innovation framework includes (i) investing in culture change; (ii) investing in staff members' and DMC counterparts' innovation skills; (iii) developing business processes for innovative projects and initiatives; (iv) forging new partnerships, especially with innovation leaders in industry, academia, and DMCs; and (v) measuring ADB's innovation capabilities and outputs.

[20]   A country team is composed of staff members at a resident mission and staff members at headquarters or at other offices in the country.

staff positions.[21] Resident missions must have a stronger role in vetting the knowledge programs developed by the regional and other departments and support peer-to-peer learning between DMCs. The review of ADB's resident mission operations provides concrete actions that link with the KMAP (Appendix 5, see footnotes).[22]

Box 8: Better Country Knowledge Programming, Sounder Country Partnership Strategies

Strategy 2030 calls for strengthening the country-focused approach and promoting knowledge management in Asian Development Bank (ADB) operations. By refining the country knowledge program as part of the country partnership strategy, ADB seeks to provide developing member countries (DMCs) with demand-responsive knowledge solutions.

The country knowledge program is the backbone of the country partnership strategy. After an assessment of the country's knowledge needs during the strategy period, the program details how ADB will meet current and future knowledge needs through a set of results and outcomes, in keeping with country and ADB priorities.

Departing from the traditional menu of knowledge products, services, and solutions, the updated country knowledge program introduces a dynamic mechanism for delivering demand-driven knowledge. The program aligns all of ADB's knowledge work with client services. ADB consultations with governments ensure that the knowledge options offered are coordinated, collaborative, and demand responsive.

The knowledge outcomes can be classified into three:

(i) increased awareness and evidence-based information, including flagship products, technical studies, working papers, and communication support for policy dialogue;
(ii) better program and project delivery, including policy support, sector technical assistance, project feasibility studies, guidance notes and toolkits, and case study and innovation notes on project and program design and implementation; and
(iii) improved capacity and skills, including knowledge partnerships and collaborations, trainings, workshops and conferences, study trips, expert visits, and knowledge exchanges to build long-term capacity and strengthen institutions.

Once a DMC's knowledge needs are classified, ADB can plan for strategic impact and understand its own comparative advantage. The objective is to provide strategic, long-term, and just-in-time knowledge and to strengthen links with the lending portfolio. A dynamic country knowledge program's outcomes make it easier to monitor progress during the country partnership strategy period and through the annual country operations business plan, where individual knowledge products and services can be listed for each outcome. As of February 2021, Mongolia, the Philippines, and Viet Nam had adopted this approach.

Source: Asian Development Bank.

---

21 The Strategy, Policy and Partnerships Department (SPD)–led country partnership strategy review paper recommends ways to strengthen country knowledge programming. ADB. 2021. *Country Partnership Strategy and Results Framework Review.* Manila.
22 ADB. 2020. *Review of ADB's Resident Mission Operations.* Manila, provides a 3-year action plan. The KMAP is aligned with it.

Silos continue to limit cross-department collaboration and learning. The digital agenda can partly solve the problem. ADB stands to gain from maximizing the benefits of advanced technology to make collaboration more widespread and agile; better manage (dispose, retain, and archive) records with business value; and deliver and apply knowledge in real time.[23] ADB can benefit from creating a connected enterprise knowledge network from which staff members can access information about all aspects of ADB operations, particularly the work in DMCs. Access can be improved by, for example, (i) leveraging existing knowledge management platforms (such as k-Nexus), and (ii) strengthening the role of sector and thematic groups to expand knowledge networks—virtual and physical—to ensure that knowledge is harvested and curated using the appropriate platforms and digital tools. In a time of information and knowledge overload, knowledge must be curated and filtered and made available to staff members and clients by using technology and the skills of the sector and thematic groups and other expert communities.

To tailor knowledge solutions to client needs, ADB seeks to strengthen knowledge management processes to guide teams in identifying relevant and quality knowledge products and services, and to allow sufficient time to transfer tacit knowledge through learning, debriefing knowledge holders, and codifying the knowledge.[24] Departments' knowledge management functions need to be carried out by dedicated teams and explicit functions within teams, which will be formed by training existing staff members and/or repurposing vacant positions. The teams serve as knowledge brokers, connectors, knowledge journalists who document tacit knowledge from teams, relationship managers, silo breakers, role models, and change makers. The development of sector and thematic learning programs and country knowledge exchange should be better coordinated through after-action reviews, case study discussions, and improved peer review, among others.

Pillar 3: Strengthen relationships. A strong knowledge network is key to ensuring that the bank taps the knowledge of its staff members (all of whom are knowledge workers in their own right) and external partners to collaborate on solutions that are timely, relevant, and sustainable. ADB's substantial reliance on consultants means it needs to better utilize, leverage, and codify knowledge and ensure that they are included in ADB's knowledge management business processes.

To ensure that it strengthens and diversifies its country, regional, and global partnerships, ADB must create clear accountability and improve processes to co-create relevant and timely knowledge solutions with knowledge partners. ADB will thereby cement the importance of engaging in and creating strategic and efficient knowledge partnerships. Think tanks are important in informing policy analysis. ADB will design and adopt flexible models to establish results-oriented partnerships across various institutions within and outside DMCs, including civil society organizations, and the private sector (Box 9).

The resident missions have a comparative advantage in building enduring relationships with key DMC stakeholders and should lead in building strong local knowledge networks. Resident missions proactively engage with civil society, academia, and the private sector, particularly to prepare country partnership strategies. Resident missions need better processes for identifying the best partners, streamlining cumbersome procedures, and maximizing relationships.

---

[23] ADB. 2020. Information Classification. *Administrative Orders.* AO 4.17. Manila.
[24] The socialization, externalization, combination, and internalization model of Ikujiro Nonaka, further refined by Hirotaka Takeuchi, describes the cycle of tacit and explicit knowledge flow and capture. I. Nonaka and H. Takeuchi. 1995. *The Knowledge-Creating Company: How Japanese Companies Create the Dynamics of Innovation.* Oxford: Oxford University Press.

Box 9: Leveraging Knowledge Partnerships

The Asian Development Bank (ADB) has forged many knowledge partnerships. Until recently, however, no unified database provided an overview of all partnerships, their strategic intent, and their impact. In 2019, ADB set up the Knowledge Partnership Database—the Toolbox—as a one-stop shop where staff members can easily find ADB's knowledge partners. The Toolbox also provides templates and guides to make building of partnerships seamless and easy. Since its roll-out, communication between knowledge partners has increased as has the sharing of compelling stories of collaboration with external partners. It is designed to systemize ADB's approach to building strategic partnerships and to expand knowledge networks.

Source: Asian Development Bank.

To expand field expertise and strengthen the capacity of frontline staff members to deliver knowledge solutions, ADB must rethink the range of skills needed to enable country teams and resident missions to build and manage relationships. Drawing from the recommendations and action plan of the review of ADB's resident mission operations, knowledge management in resident missions will include, among others, (i) sharpening their role as client and program teams, (ii) focusing on deeper diagnostics to advance knowledge of the country context, and (iii) refining the country focus of knowledge operations. These actions will allow ADB to maintain its cutting-edge understanding of country issues; develop the best solutions to meet development needs (including integrated solutions); and help strengthen relationships with the private sector, academia, civil society, and other organizations. The KMAP will build on knowledge management achievements, which showcase a structured approach to internal and external capacity development, working closely with the ADB Institute's capacity as an outstanding think tank, capturing and sharing tacit knowledge, and transferring and applying knowledge (Box 10).

Strengthening relationships between ADB functions and fostering a "One ADB" approach requires agility, collaboration, and a concerted effort to mobilize responses to knowledge needs from key players in the bank. ADB will review and reconfirm the roles of key actors (country directors and resident missions, sector directors and sector divisions, sector and thematic groups, among others) in responding holistically to clients, developing and managing portfolios, and strengthening the new ADB client management system.

Nurturing relationships with international financial institutions and other intergovernmental organizations on knowledge management will enable ADB to benefit from good practices on managing knowledge through continuous learning. The organizations and ADB can partner on knowledge initiatives. Building such a knowledge collaboration network will strengthen ADB's own focus on knowledge work.

Box 10: Managing Knowledge Captured from Working with Civil Society

The NGO and Civil Society Center (NGOC) of the Asian Development Bank (ADB) helps project officers engage with civil society organizations (CSOs). In Uzbekistan, for example, NGOC helps three projects—one each for agriculture and natural resources, transport, and water—involve local organizations in project delivery. NGOC joins project and country teams across ADB to show how CSOs can add value to projects and how ADB teams can build relationships with CSOs. NGOC helps ADB staff members identify ADB resources for CSO engagement and pinpoint CSO and youth partners.

NGOC brings the voices of civil society to ADB through brownbag speakers and training programs. CSOs are a source of innovation, such as the Building Resources Across Communities (BRAC)– designed graduation approach to poverty reduction, which ADB now incorporates into some of its lending. NGOC's annual training program, which reaches more than 60 staff members each year, provides an opportunity for dialogue with civil society representatives and ADB management. The civil society program of the annual meeting is a much larger platform that promotes CSO participation.

NGOC is building a resource center on its digital community site, which includes a wide range of ADB publications on civil society engagement. They include civil society briefs; NGOC's flagship publication, which presents the civil society landscape in selected developing member countries; guidance on participating in and working with CSOs; social media feeds highlighting good practice in CSO engagement; Participation Tools for the Pacific; and a suite of three training courses on working with CSOs, available to ADB staff members, CSOs, and government officials.

NGOC continues to expand its knowledge repository. For example, it is discussing with the Lao People's Democratic Republic country team how it can host a database on CSOs.

Source: Asian Development Bank.

IV. IMPLEMENTATION ARRANGEMENTS AND MONITORING

As the KMAP has implications for everyone's work in the organization, its implementation will be the responsibility of all departments and offices (Figure 2).

The KMAP's proposed implementation arrangements have five primary features:

(i) **Role of departments and their knowledge management focal points.** Departments are responsible for implementing the KMAP. A small group in each department should be designated as focal point for knowledge management and will support and monitor KMAP implementation. The group of knowledge focal points will be trained to advise on knowledge management tools, best practices, communication, and effective knowledge application and transfer. Each department will formulate its own road map (Appendix 6) and develop differentiated approaches to execute the KMAP's principles and adapt the actions.[25] The group coordinating the action plan of the review of ADB's resident mission operations, led by the Strategy, Policy, and Partnerships Department and the Budget, People, and Management Systems Department, will support and monitor the KMAP resident mission–related actions. The Strategy 2030 implementation group will monitor and tackle related key implementation issues.

(ii) **Role of the knowledge management group.** The mandate of the existing knowledge management group in departments under the Office of the Vice-President for Knowledge Management is proposed to be expanded.[26] The group will coordinate KMAP implementation across the bank, serve as a clearinghouse to ensure synergies for bank-wide reforms and initiatives, and report on best knowledge management practices and on progress to senior management and the Office of the President through the Strategy 2030 implementation group.[27] The Knowledge Advisory Services Center of the Sustainable Development and Climate Change Department (SDCC-KC)

---

[25] A model will develop and test examples of how to use knowledge management tools to benefit clients.

[26] The group has consisted of senior staff members from the Department of Communications, the Economic Research and Regional Cooperation Department, the Sustainable Development and Climate Change Department, and the Office of the Vice-President for Knowledge Management and Sustainable Development.

[27] The group was established in December 2019 to promote collaboration across departments, facilitate exchange of ideas between different business lines on key strategic initiatives, and serve as a high-level platform for corporate change management. The group consists of the heads of the operations departments; the Sustainable Development and Climate Change Department; the Information Technology Department; the Procurement, Portfolio and Financial Management Department; and the Budget, People, and Management Systems Department, and is led by the head of the Strategy, Policy and Partnerships Department.

Figure 2: Knowledge Management Action Plan Implementation Arrangements and Reporting

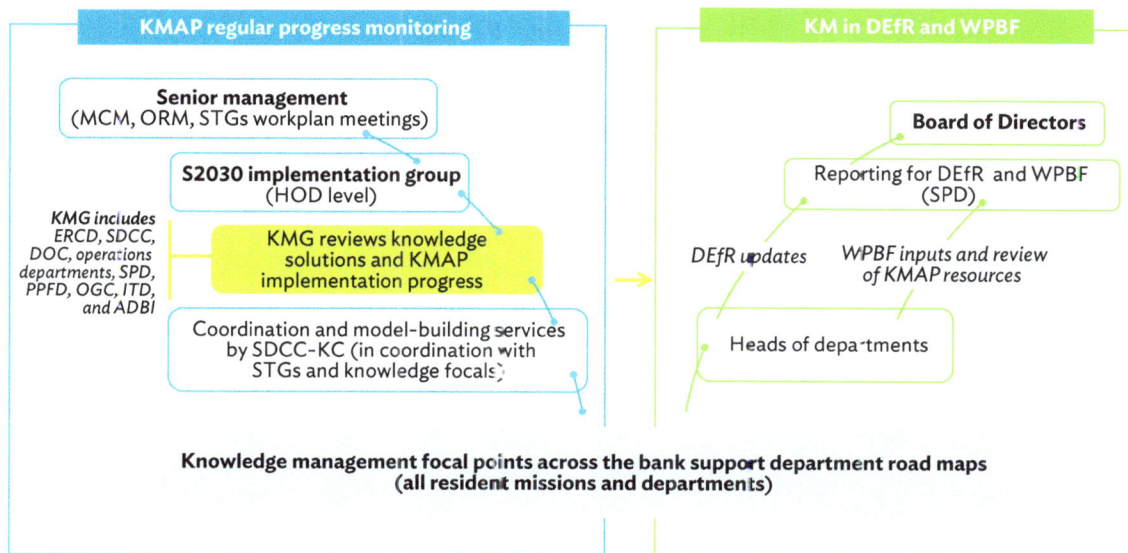

KMAP regular progress monitoring

Senior management
(MCM, ORM, STGs workplan meetings)

S2030 implementation group
(HOD level)

KMG includes ERCD, SDCC, DOC, operations departments, SPD, PPFD, OGC, ITD, and ADBI

KMG reviews knowledge solutions and KMAP implementation progress

Coordination and model-building services by SDCC-KC (in coordination with STGs and knowledge focals)

KM in DEfR and WPBF

Board of Directors

Reporting for DEfR and WPBF (SPD)

DEfR updates   *WPBF inputs and review of KMAP resources*

Heads of departments

**Knowledge management focal points across the bank support department road maps
(all resident missions and departments)**

DOC = Department of Communications; DEfR = development effectiveness review; ERCD = Economic Research and Regional Cooperation Department; HOD = head of department; ITD = Information Technology Department; SDCC-KC = Knowledge Advisory Services Center, Sustainable Development and Climate Change Department; KMAP = Knowledge Management Action Plan; KMG = knowledge management group; MCM = management committee meeting; ORM = operations review meeting; PPFD = Procurement, Portfolio and Financial Management Department; S2030 = Strategy 2030; SPD = Strategy, Policy and Partnerships Department; STGs = sector and thematic groups; WPBF = work program and budget framework.

Source: Asian Development Bank.

will be the secretariat for the knowledge management group and coordinate with and support entities across ADB that are implementing reforms and their KMAP road maps. SDCC-KC will support country knowledge programming, lead new ways of strengthening collaboration, improve strategic engagement with knowledge partners, and feature knowledge management best practices and innovation to change behavior.

(iii) **Work program and budget framework and development effectiveness review.** To keep transaction costs of implementing and monitoring the KMAP to a minimum, existing reporting mechanisms will be used. Through the work program and budget framework (WPBF), departments inform the Board of the scope of their operations and quantitative and qualitative knowledge work.[28] Reporting on the progress in meeting the Corporate Results Framework requirements as part of the annual development effectiveness review (DEfR) will ensure that headway in attaining knowledge results is

---

[28] The WPBF analyzes elements of knowledge work contained in, for example, technical assistance operations (new commitments and number of knowledge and support technical assistance projects), department knowledge products, knowledge solutions, staffing requirements (including experts increasingly used to generate and share knowledge in key sectors and thematic areas), and building of sector and thematic knowledge. The WPBF provides a comprehensive picture of, among others, knowledge work as integral to ADB operations.

communicated to the Board.[29] The mechanisms combine quantitative and qualitative data from the client and staff surveys. Additional staff survey questions will be designed to capture staff behavior and satisfaction related to knowledge management. The KMAP includes a results framework composed of indicators from the Corporate Results Framework and the client and staff surveys (Appendix 2).

(iv) **Results monitoring and action tracking.** Part of DEfR reporting entails seeking DMCs' feedback to measure the effect of ADB's knowledge work and client satisfaction. The reporting will draw upon the results of the biennial client survey (baseline data are available as of 2018 and will be available again in 2021). The Department of Communications will continue to monitor dissemination of ADB's published knowledge work. The staff survey will monitor staff behavior and satisfaction. The participation of knowledge partners and experts, including technical advisory groups, in reviewing and giving feedback on the quality of key knowledge products and services will be expanded.[30] The KMAP will be tracked annually, with status updates provided for all ongoing actions. The impact of improved knowledge management is increased efficiency, quality, and innovation. Since ADB is a noncommercial entity, its business volume is not the only appropriate indicator. The KMAP will monitor how ADB advances policy dialogue and whether projects help achieve the Sustainable Development Goals in line with Strategy 2030 targets.

(v) **Reporting to senior management.** Staff members will regularly report on progress and emerging issues in executing the KMAP at management committee meetings, operational review meetings, and sector and thematic group workplan discussions, and to the Strategy 2030 implementation group.

KMAP implementation arrangements are designed to reduce departments' reporting transaction costs and to maximize reporting on (i) knowledge results in achievements and client satisfaction (through the DEfR to the Board, with information channeled through existing means); (ii) knowledge work that is part of the work program of departments and its alignment across ADB with Strategy 2030 (through the WPBF to the Board, using existing channels); and (iii) knowledge solutions and reports on issues of KMAP implementation (via efforts of the knowledge management group, with SDCC-KC secretariat services, and through reporting mechanisms to senior management).

KMAP implementation is planned in three phases (Figure 3): (i) phase one—align ADB's knowledge management efforts with the KMAP's principles and action plan, (ii) phase 2—customize approaches and improve good-practice models, and (ii) phase 3—mainstream these practices and models across the bank. All three phases are underpinned by culture change, talent management, and innovation.

---

[29] ADB. 2019. *ADB Corporate Results Framework, 2019–2024*. Manila. The framework has 10 knowledge indicators grouped into four categories: knowledge delivered, used, and benefiting clients; and ADB's readiness to become a better knowledge organization. Of the 10 indicators, 2 are results framework indicators with baselines and targets, and 8 are tracking indicators; 7 are harmonized with those of other multilateral development banks. The KMAP will provide additional indicators to monitor progress in line with the Theory of Change. The Corporate Results Framework midterm review, planned for 2021, will provide an opportunity to adjust the framework's knowledge indicators.

[30] Several sector and thematic groups, such as the Climate Change and Disaster Risk Management Thematic Group, are already identifying external reviewers for all knowledge products to ensure high quality and relevance.

Figure 3: Knowledge Management Action Plan Implementation Phases

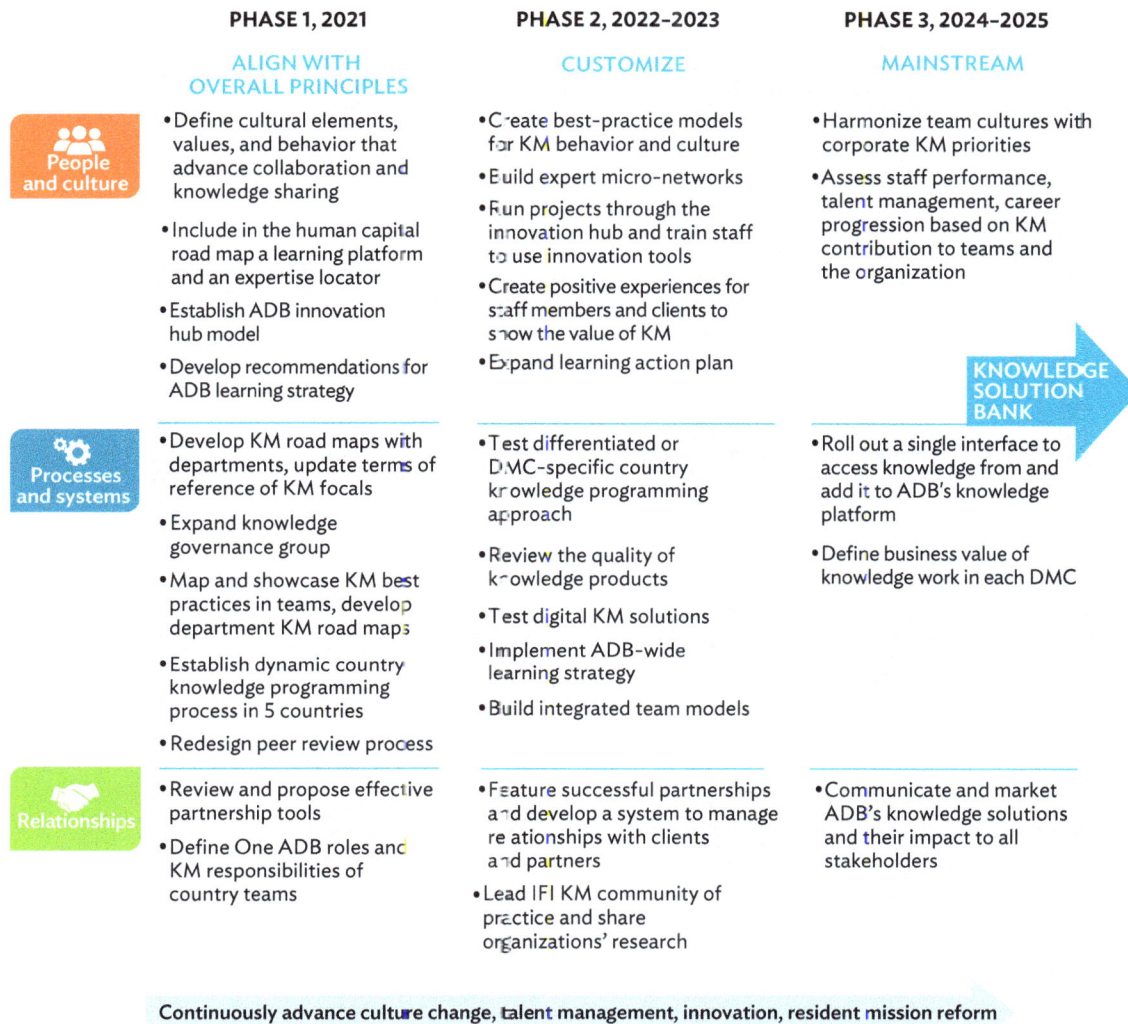

	PHASE 1, 2021 ALIGN WITH OVERALL PRINCIPLES	PHASE 2, 2022–2023 CUSTOMIZE	PHASE 3, 2024–2025 MAINSTREAM
People and culture	• Define cultural elements, values, and behavior that advance collaboration and knowledge sharing • Include in the human capital road map a learning platform and an expertise locator • Establish ADB innovation hub model • Develop recommendations for ADB learning strategy	• Create best-practice models for KM behavior and culture • Build expert micro-networks • Run projects through the innovation hub and train staff to use innovation tools • Create positive experiences for staff members and clients to show the value of KM • Expand learning action plan	• Harmonize team cultures with corporate KM priorities • Assess staff performance, talent management, career progression based on KM contribution to teams and the organization
Processes and systems	• Develop KM road maps with departments, update terms of reference of KM focals • Expand knowledge governance group • Map and showcase KM best practices in teams, develop department KM road maps • Establish dynamic country knowledge programming process in 5 countries • Redesign peer review process	• Test differentiated or DMC-specific country knowledge programming approach • Review the quality of knowledge products • Test digital KM solutions • Implement ADB-wide learning strategy • Build integrated team models	**KNOWLEDGE SOLUTION BANK** • Roll out a single interface to access knowledge from and add it to ADB's knowledge platform • Define business value of knowledge work in each DMC
Relationships	• Review and propose effective partnership tools • Define One ADB roles and KM responsibilities of country teams	• Feature successful partnerships and develop a system to manage relationships with clients and partners • Lead IFI KM community of practice and share organizations' research	• Communicate and market ADB's knowledge solutions and their impact to all stakeholders

Continuously advance culture change, talent management, innovation, resident mission reform

ADB = Asian Development Bank, DMC = developing member country, IFI = international financial institution, KM = knowledge management, KMAP = Knowledge Management Action Plan.

Source: Asian Development Bank.

A.   Providing Resources

ISO 30401 (section 7.1., Resources) states that to provide resources to a knowledge management system, four elements need to be considered: funding, workforce, technology, and management commitment. To this list can be added an organizational culture that motivates staff members to take on change management. Technology and management commitment are difficult to quantify but crucial to understand how ADB can support the KMAP.[31] Knowledge

---

[31]   Well-defined methodologies to ascertain "management commitment" and "openness to change management" are generally lacking. However, they are critical to understanding the amount of resources ADB needs to implement the KMAP. Both elements have become increasingly visible in ADB in recent years, and their contribution to helping meet the KMAP objectives should not be underestimated.

work and knowledge management are financed through staff time, administrative budget for staff consultants, service providers, technical assistance resources, and loan and grant projects that can fund capacity development and knowledge sharing and capture. The existing ADB experts pool is a unique source of knowledge work and organizational learning. As knowledge work is integral to all departments' operations and covers all areas (sector and thematic), determining the exact level of resources dedicated to knowledge work is not feasible. The closest proxies for such calculations are the following:[32]

(i) **Total size of technical assistance** for knowledge generation and sharing, innovation, project preparation and implementation, and DMC capacity development. For example, during the 2020–2022 WPBF, projected technical assistance commitments total $1.3 billion (or an average of $428 million per year, in contrast to an average of actual commitments of $336 million during the 2016–2018 WPBF).

(ii) **Level of the Technical Assistance Special Fund**, up from $594 million actual commitment in 2016–2018 to a projected commitment of $649 million in 2020–2022, of which $96 million is allocated to upper-middle-income countries.[33] Some of these resources are earmarked for strengthening departments' coordination and focus of country knowledge work.

(iii) **Other special funds** (from $29 million in 2016–2018 to $128 million in 2020–2022).[34]

(iv) **Trust funds** (from $257 million in 2016–2018 to $340 million in 2020–2022).[35]

(v) **Level of staffing costs.** The WPBF for 2020–2022 stipulates that "ADB's effort to offset future staff requirements will be achieved through productivity enhancements." These include, for example, (a) sharing staff resources across departments and operations through short-term assignments, strategic staff placements, a mobility framework, and pooled experts; and (b) making greater use of flexible position management, adjusting job roles and grades, and redeploying existing staff positions across departments. Provision of resources, therefore, need not be in the form of nominal increases in staff size but opportunities to leverage networks.

The KMAP will use existing resource allocation processes strategically to seek additional resources:

(i) Many of the actions proposed in the KMAP will be cost neutral and require no or few direct resources. The actions focus on efficiency and quality improvements and rely on sensible allocation decisions.

(ii) Proactive and flexible budget management provisions have made funds fungible such that knowledge work can be financed by reallocating funds meant for the year's budget. For example, business travel allocations may be set aside for more staff consulting expenses. Costs do not increase even if knowledge work does.

(iii) The review of ADB's resident mission operations recommends better alignment of knowledge technical assistance resources with DMCs' knowledge needs and with the lending portfolio.

(iv) The skills development program for sector and thematic groups allots about $2 million annually for training programs for the 15 groups, to make better use of ADB case studies to improve the flow, transfer, and capture of tacit knowledge and lessons learned.

---

[32] ADB. 2019. *Work Program and Budget Framework, 2020–2022.* Manila.

[33] The Technical Assistance Special Fund supports, among others, knowledge sharing among DMCs and in areas where countries have limited domestic expertise, such as advanced technology; emerging issues (e.g., aging population); and public–private partnership legal frameworks.

[34] Other special funds include the Japan Special Fund and the Financial Sector Development Partnership Special Fund.

[35] Trust funds are used for investment projects and technical assistance for capacity development; project preparation, including detailed design; and knowledge work. As of mid-2019, ADB had administered 47 trust funds, of which 34 were active.

Figure 4: Providing Resources for the Knowledge Management Action Plan

	No additional cost Integral to existing mandates and initiatives	Cost neutral Efficiency measures that mobilize existing budgets	Additional cost One-time costs to increase productivity
People and culture	• Launch of culture transformation initiative • KM capacity development		• Human capital road map • Implementation of culture change
Processes and systems	• Department KM road maps • Country knowledge programming • Expansion of country teams • Existing systems upgraded and made interoperable	• Improved peer review and KM as part of business processes • Strengthened KM capacity with explicit functions	• Bolstered KM capacity with explicit functions in country teams
Relationships	• Client relationship management system	• Reinforced partnerships	

KM = knowledge management.

Source: Asian Development Bank.

(v) The staff development program, managed by the Budget, People, and Management Systems Department (about $7 million a year), funds leadership development, management skills, e-learning, personal growth, coaching, external learning programs, membership in professional associations, and business skills.

(vi) The digital agenda sets funds aside for change management and skills development in information technology use and includes the preparation of a human capital road map.

Prioritizing and phasing actions can inform options to provide resources to implement the KMAP (Figure 4).

B.   Assessment

A midterm assessment of the KMAP is proposed in the first half of 2023 to improve its implementation. The assessment will be done in collaboration with departments that will be represented in the expanded knowledge management group. The report will be presented to senior management and for information to the Board with recommendations for additional measures that may be required. A comprehensive stocktaking of examples of knowledge management practices in ADB is ongoing and will guide all ADB teams. The stocktaking will continue and share best practices. A final assessment of the KMAP implementation will be conducted in early 2026 to inform the next KMAP.

APPENDIXES

APPENDIX 1

Knowledge Management Cycle

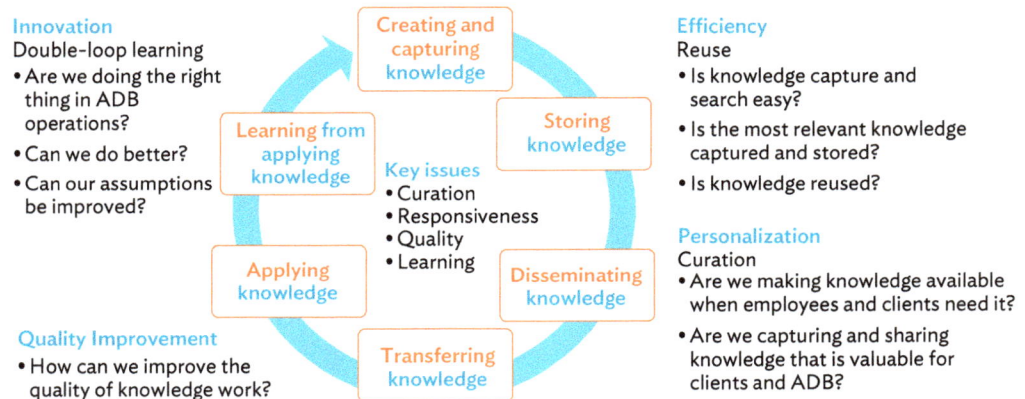

Innovation
Double-loop learning
- Are we doing the right thing in ADB operations?
- Can we do better?
- Can our assumptions be improved?

Quality Improvement
- How can we improve the quality of knowledge work?

Key issues
- Curation
- Responsiveness
- Quality
- Learning

Creating and capturing knowledge
Storing knowledge
Disseminating knowledge
Transferring knowledge
Applying knowledge
Learning from applying knowledge

Efficiency
Reuse
- Is knowledge capture and search easy?
- Is the most relevant knowledge captured and stored?
- Is knowledge reused?

Personalization
Curation
- Are we making knowledge available when employees and clients need it?
- Are we capturing and sharing knowledge that is valuable for clients and ADB?

ADB = Asian Development Bank.

Source: Adapted from K. Dalkir. 2011. *Knowledge Management in Theory and Practice.* Second edition. Cambridge, MA: MIT Press.

APPENDIX 2

Knowledge Management Action Plan Results Framework and Its Alignment with the Theory of Change and the Corporate Results Framework

	Results Statements	Indicators	Data Source
Long-term results	Improved development results in Asia and the Pacific		
Medium-term results	1. Better-informed policies, programs, projects, and operations in DMCs	1.A. Clients benefiting from ADB's contribution to DMC policy, programs, projects, and operations (%)	Client survey–new
		1.B. Clients satisfied with ADB's development effectiveness in helping them achieve results (%)	Client survey–CRF
		1.C. Completed technical assistance projects rated successful (%)	Administrative data
		1.E. Event participants reporting increased knowledge and/or skills (number)	Administrative data
	2. Improved recognition of ADB as a leading and trusted regional knowledge solutions provider	2.A. Clients describing ADB as trustworthy (%)	Client survey–new
		2.B. Client rating on comparative quality of ADB knowledge products and services (%)	Client survey–new
		2.C. Client rating on comparative dissemination effectiveness of ADB knowledge products and services (%)	Client survey–new
		2.D. Clients satisfied with the use of ADB knowledge products (%)	Client survey–CRF
	3. Increased flow of DMC-tailored knowledge solutions	3.A. Web-distributed knowledge solutions (number of downloads)	Administrative data
		3.B. Engagement on social media (number)	Administrative data
		3.C. Quality rating of knowledge expert panels and/or technical advisory groups on key selected knowledge solutions (%)	Independent panel review–new
		3.D. Client rating on ADB's performance in providing integrated solutions (%) (new)	Client survey–new
		3.E. Client rating on alignment of ADB's technical assistance operations with DMC national development priorities (%) (new)	Client survey–new
		3.F. Innovative operations and technical assistance project (%)	Administrative data

continued on next page

Table continued

	Results Statements	Indicators	Data Source
Intermediate results	**Pillar 1. People and culture** Improving institutional culture to incentivize, create, and promote knowledge solutions	1.1. Staff reporting improved practices in knowledge management (%)	Staff survey–new
		1.2. Staff rating ADB as providing enabling culture for Strategy 2030 implementation (%)	Administrative data
		1.3. Staff rating ADB as an effective knowledge and learning organization (%)	Staff survey–CRF
	Pillar 2. Processes and systems Strengthening ADB processes and systems for client-oriented knowledge creation, flow, and use	2.1. Staff satisfied with ease of finding and capturing knowledge (%)	Staff survey–new
		2.2. Client rating on the efficiency of ADB's delivery of technical assistance (%)	Client survey–new
		2.3. Validated ratings of relevance of ADB's country assistance programs (%)	Administrative data
		2.4. Knowledge products and services drawn from k-Nexus (number)	Administrative data
	Pillar 3. Relationships Strengthening ADB's knowledge partnerships and relationships	3.1. Staff rating on effectiveness of ADB's internal collaboration (%)	Staff survey–new
		3.2. Staff rating on effectiveness of ADB's external partnerships (%)	Staff survey–new
		3.3. Stakeholders satisfied with ADB's collaboration with development partners (%)	Client survey–CRF
		3.4. Clients satisfied with ADB's responsiveness to meeting their needs (%)	Client survey–CRF

ADB = Asian Development Bank, CRF = Corporate Results Framework, DMC = developing member country.
Source: Asian Development Bank.

Alignment of Results Indicators with Theory of Change

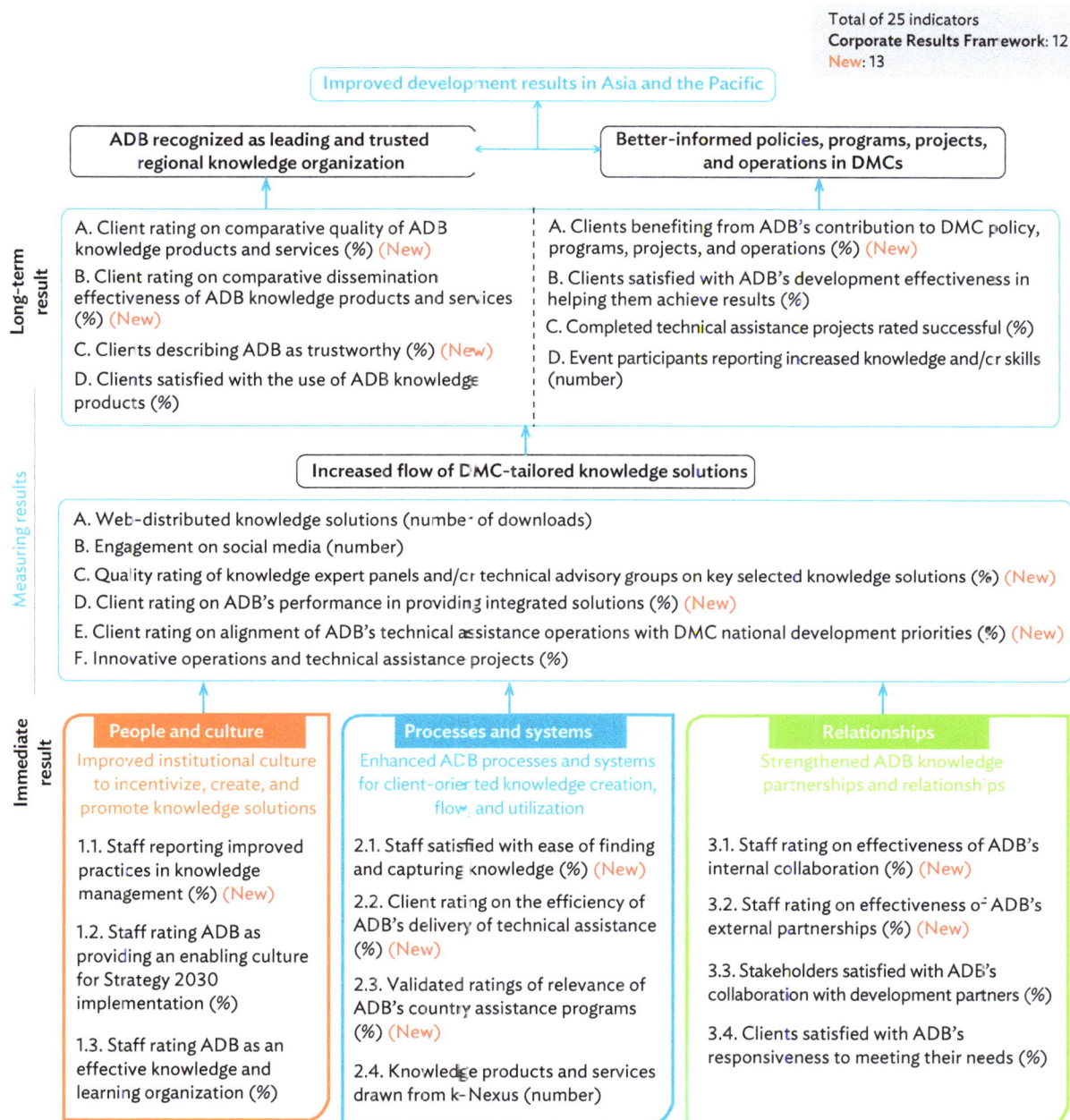

Total of 25 indicators
Corporate Results Framework: 12
New: 13

Improved development results in Asia and the Pacific

ADB recognized as leading and trusted regional knowledge organization

Better-informed policies, programs, projects, and operations in DMCs

Long-term result

A. Client rating on comparative quality of ADB knowledge products and services (%) (New)

B. Client rating on comparative dissemination effectiveness of ADB knowledge products and services (%) (New)

C. Clients describing ADB as trustworthy (%) (New)

D. Clients satisfied with the use of ADB knowledge products (%)

A. Clients benefiting from ADB's contribution to DMC policy, programs, projects, and operations (%) (New)

B. Clients satisfied with ADB's development effectiveness in helping them achieve results (%)

C. Completed technical assistance projects rated successful (%)

D. Event participants reporting increased knowledge and/or skills (number)

Measuring results

Increased flow of DMC-tailored knowledge solutions

A. Web-distributed knowledge solutions (number of downloads)

B. Engagement on social media (number)

C. Quality rating of knowledge expert panels and/or technical advisory groups on key selected knowledge solutions (%) (New)

D. Client rating on ADB's performance in providing integrated solutions (%) (New)

E. Client rating on alignment of ADB's technical assistance operations with DMC national development priorities (%) (New)

F. Innovative operations and technical assistance projects (%)

Immediate result

People and culture
Improved institutional culture to incentivize, create, and promote knowledge solutions

1.1. Staff reporting improved practices in knowledge management (%) (New)

1.2. Staff rating ADB as providing an enabling culture for Strategy 2030 implementation (%)

1.3. Staff rating ADB as an effective knowledge and learning organization (%)

Processes and systems
Enhanced ADB processes and systems for client-oriented knowledge creation, flow, and utilization

2.1. Staff satisfied with ease of finding and capturing knowledge (%) (New)

2.2. Client rating on the efficiency of ADB's delivery of technical assistance (%) (New)

2.3. Validated ratings of relevance of ADB's country assistance programs (%) (New)

2.4. Knowledge products and services drawn from k-Nexus (number)

Relationships
Strengthened ADB knowledge partnerships and relationships

3.1. Staff rating on effectiveness of ADB's internal collaboration (%) (New)

3.2. Staff rating on effectiveness of ADB's external partnerships (%) (New)

3.3. Stakeholders satisfied with ADB's collaboration with development partners (%)

3.4. Clients satisfied with ADB's responsiveness to meeting their needs (%)

ADB = Asian Development Bank, DMC = developing member country.
Source: Asian Development Bank.

APPENDIX 3

Examples of Knowledge Solutions

In 2019, the Asian Development Bank (ADB) started collecting knowledge solutions from its operations and other work. The initiative was the first bank-wide exercise to measure, report, and recognize how knowledge helps solve development problems faced by developing member countries (DMCs). That year, 16 departments nominated 45 diverse sets of knowledge solutions. Submissions included knowledge products (including detailed analytical reports and studies), knowledge services (such as conferences and workshops), and knowledge embedded in technical assistance projects and programs. The evidence included media citations, video blogs, and observations from DMC clients.

The submissions were validated by the knowledge management group. Most were validated by the departments. The group identified knowledge solutions as significant if they

(i) tackled a clearly identified problem,
(ii) were based on knowledge and evidence, and
(iii) were necessary and decisive in delivering development results or highly appreciated by clients and beneficiaries.

Of the submissions, 29 were assessed as significant while the rest were viewed as needing more evidence of impact and client appreciation to establish how the knowledge resolved the development challenge identified.

Examples of significant knowledge solutions are the following:

(i) **Knowledge as policy advice rendered and accepted**
   (a) Given how detrimental air pollution is to public health, the East Asia Department team recommended policies to curb air pollution in Ulaanbaatar. The policy note was part of a series of efforts to reduce air pollution by more than 40% from the winter of 2018 to the winter of 2019. Mongolian Parliament Speaker Zandanshatar Gombojav cited the policy note when he assigned working groups to curb air pollution and the cabinet to improve measures to combat air pollution and to strengthen the engagement of the private sector, civil society, media companies, and international organizations in the effort. The speaker ordered officials to study medium- and long-term recommendations in a policy note, Winning the Fight Against Air Pollution in Ulaanbaatar, and to implement the policy actions consistently.

   (b) Following decades of underinvestment in education, weak human capital threatens to trap Myanmar in an economic model based on cheap, unskilled labor and natural resource exploitation, undermining poverty reduction and inclusive growth. The Southeast Asia Department supported analysis, policy and planning, capacity development for post-primary education, and pilot testing of technical and vocational education and training programs to equip disadvantaged youth with skills urgently demanded in the labor market. The support helped the Ministry of Education formulate its National Education Strategic Plan for secondary education and technical and vocational education and training.

(c) The Regional Cooperation and Integration Thematic Group of the Sustainable Development and Climate Change Department worked with the Pacific Department on a study of opportunities for and challenges to reducing poverty in neglected border regions to boost trade and cooperation between Indonesia and Timor-Leste. The study informed and expedited the signing of a memorandum of understanding between them on cross-border cooperation. As committed to in the memorandum, the Timor-Leste government allowed Indonesian tourists to enter Timor-Leste without a visa.

(d) Depleting groundwater resources in and around Dhaka raised the need to tap new sources of surface water. An ADB project explored the potential of the Meghna River as an alternative water source. As the river faces serious pollution threats, a 2019 South Asia Department report, *Protecting the Meghna River—A Sustainable Water Resource for Dhaka*, recommended designating ecologically critical areas, promoting cleaner industrial production, monitoring pollution, controlling wastewater discharge and pesticide use, and empowering local stewardship of the river. The Dhaka Water Supply and Sewerage Authority and its Department of Environment are keen to implement the recommendations. Otherwise, additional treatment would cost about $175.3 million annually if the river water quality deteriorated further.

(ii) **Knowledge solutions that demonstrated the use of evidence**
   (a) Informed by a 2015 urban assessment and an integrated urban planning and regional development process in 2016, a $15 million loan to Georgia will finance the preparation and design of the Livable Cities Investment Program. It will make cities more accessible and inclusive, with better solid waste management, small and medium-sized enterprise development, and women's entrepreneurship. The program was led by the Central and West Asia Department and multiple sector and thematic groups.

   (b) In the absence of quantifiable information to understand market gaps in trade finance and their impact, the Private Sector Operations Department and the Economic Research and Regional Cooperation Department prepared the Trade Finance Gaps, Growth, and Jobs Survey. It aims to (i) identify market gaps in trade finance, (ii) understand why gaps exist, (iii) explain their impact on growth and jobs, and (iv) identify actions to close the gaps. The study is the first of its kind and has been cited by institutions and publications, including *The Economist and The Financial Times*. The study recommends that governments adopt common laws as well as a legal entity identifier. A unique electronic 20-digit identifier for legal entities participating in financial and commercial transactions would help combat money laundering and encourage knowing the customer.

(iii) **Knowledge solutions that use high-level technology**
   (a) The $1.5 billion Shandong Green Development Fund helps decarbonize the province and supports the nationally determined contribution of peaking carbon emissions by 2030. The climate fund is the first in the People's Republic of China (PRC) that integrates gender equality into financing. The project promotes a green procurement framework and uses digital platforms to improve the preparation of high-quality infrastructure projects and to monitor the fund's financial and climate

targets. ADB is scaling up the initiative nationally through the Ministry of Ecology and Environment in the PRC, and in Southeast Asia and Mongolia.

(b)   Extremely remote, vulnerable to climate change, weak in governance, and categorized since 2008 as a fragile and conflict-affected situation, Nauru lacked the institutional and human resource capacity and experience necessary for effective, efficient, quality project preparation and implementation. To solve these problems, ADB mobilized technical assistance and projects to engage independent design reviewers to advise the government on project design, probity experts to fully audit project procurement, and an independent technical auditor to ensure compliance with technical and safeguard standards. ADB used digital twin technology supported by drones to monitor projects.

(c)   The rapid adoption of smart devices and the accompanying change in readership habits from print to digital encouraged ADB to explore new ways of reaching its audience. The ADB annual report digital file is among the most downloaded products on ADB's website. The addition of the Smart Reader version was expected to lead to a decrease in the number of PDF downloads. The Smart Reader has significantly expanded the audience for the annual report, bringing in thousands of new readers, while the PDF downloads have remained consistent with previous years. As of 31 December 2019, the Smart Reader had attracted 4,791 mobile users.

APPENDIX 4

Knowledge Management Tools

Underpinned by incentives for knowledge management

Capital (employees can increase their value),
motivation (role models), policy

People

- Meetings, workshops, conferences, webinars
- Knowledge mentorships
- Informal exchanges
- Best-practice sharing: exchanges, publications, field trips, study tours
- Seminars on lessons learned
- Storytelling, knowledge maps

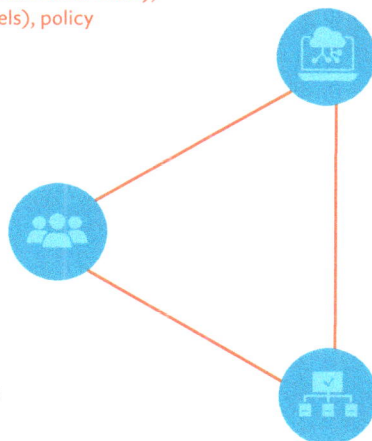

Systems, technology

- Document management system
- Content management system
- Group software (e.g., MS 360) for cooperation and communication
- E-learning platforms
- Digital knowledge maps
- Social software
- Portals
- Digital community sites, staff directories, expert locator systems

Processes, organizations, relationships

- Responsibilities, provision of resources for knowledge management
- Job rotations
- Knowledge planning methods, such as work process analysis
- Integration of client knowledge
- Communities of practice, knowledge assessment methods
- Open culture for knowledge sharing and collaboration, diversity

Source: Asian Development Bank.

APPENDIX 5

Proposed Knowledge Management Action Plan Actions

Theory of Change: Pillars and Actions to Achieve Desired Results	Responsibility
PILLAR 1: PEOPLE AND CULTURE **1. Align the KMAP with culture transformation initiatives.** ADB needs to align its incentives with the new values and enable Strategy 2030.	
1.1. Align the KMAP with culture transformation initiatives embracing collaboration and knowledge promotion.	**Lead:** BPMSD, SPD, SDCC **Support:** All departments
1.2. Articulate new values and associated behaviors and integrate them into human resource practices, systems, and business processes to reinforce changes expedited and sustained over time.	**Lead:** BPMSD **Support:** All departments
1.3. Include building an enabling culture for knowledge and innovation in leadership development and coaching programs.	**Lead:** BPMSD **Support:** All departments
2. Recruit, develop, and incentivize staff members who have relevant knowledge management competencies.	
2.1. Based on the outcome of the ADB-wide job architecture review, develop detailed knowledge management competencies, specify encouraged behaviors for each job family, and apply them in the recruitment process. This action includes updating terms of reference of department knowledge focal points and of the bank-wide knowledge management group.	**Lead:** BPMSD, SDCC **Support:** All departments
2.2. Reinforce knowledge management competencies and behaviors (e.g., collaboration and agility, lifelong learning) through the performance review and the incentive system.	**Lead:** BPMSD, SDCC **Support:** All departments
2.3. Establish a single corporate learning platform supported by a learning action plan based on ADB learning principles, so that staff members can easily access corporate, organizational, sector and thematic, digital skills, and digital workplace–specific learning programs through one portal.	**Lead:** BPMSD, SDCC, ITD **Support:** All departments
2.4. Set up or improve staff members' and consultants' profiles in the ADB system, including on sector and thematic group community sites, to locate and complement a skills–expertise matrix in line with related human resource support measures.	**Lead:** BPMSD, ITD, PPFD **Support:** All departments
2.5. Encourage and facilitate the continuous sharing, transfer, and capture of tacit knowledge among staff members and teams, particularly during times of mobility (e.g., changing roles, promotions, pending departure from ADB).	**Lead:** BPMSD
3. Implement the innovation framework.	
3.1. Put in place and carry out a change management program supported by department knowledge management focal points to foster innovation in internal processes and in development operations to make transformational change possible.	**Lead:** SPD, SDCC
3.2. Monitor and report on implementation of the innovation framework's five actions: (i) Invest in culture change. (ii) Invest in staff members' and DMC counterparts' innovation skills. (iii) Develop business processes for innovative projects and initiatives. (iv) Forge new partnerships, especially with innovation leaders in industry, academia, and DMCs. (v) Measure ADB's innovation capabilities and outputs.	**Lead:** SPD, BPMSD, SDCC **Support:** All departments
PILLAR 2: PROCESSES AND SYSTEMS **1. Strengthen country knowledge programming efforts in the country partnership strategy, to prioritize government demands and needs and target knowledge outcomes.**	
1.1. Refine country knowledge programming[a] to identify priority areas for ADB's knowledge support and develop knowledge outcomes and solutions for DMCs during preparation of country partnership strategies to support current and future lending.[b]	**Lead:** SPD **Support:** SDCC

continued on next page

Table continued

Theory of Change: Pillars and Actions to Achieve Desired Results	Responsibility
1.1.1. Apply processes and tools[c] to understand DMCs' knowledge needs, e.g., (i) rigorous quantitative and qualitative analytical work and sector and thematic assessments; (ii) participatory stakeholder knowledge consultations, including with civil society organizations; (iii) futures thinking and foresight; and (iv) training in dynamic country knowledge plans focusing on knowledge outcomes.	**Lead:** Operations departments **Support:** SDCC, ERCD
1.2. Strengthen the knowledge management capacity of resident missions to meet their knowledge needs and perform required knowledge management functions in country teams. This action includes equipping resident missions with awareness-raising and information material about the scope of ADB's knowledge work that could be relevant for DMCs.	**Lead:** Operations departments **Support:** BPMSD, SDCC
1.3. Offer knowledge management capacity-building and skills development programs to DMC entities that may request them.	**Lead:** Operations departments, PPFD **Support:** BPMSD, SDCC
2. Create a connected enterprise knowledge network where ADB staff members can access and contribute to uniform information about all sector and thematic work; new initiatives; country context; and projects, with all their consulting reports and supporting data. Make the information available across sectors, themes, and departments.	
2.1. Unleash the knowledge potential offered by the corporate deployment of the electronic document and records management system. Include knowledge management in sovereign operations modernization and digital workplace programs under the digital agenda. Use an implementation road map that specifies resource requirements and priorities.	**Lead:** SPD, ITD, OAS **Support:** Regional departments, SDCC, PPFD, ITD
2.2. Develop a long-term vision and determine the technologies for ADB's knowledge work, such as artificial intelligence–assisted knowledge management as part of the digital agenda.	**Lead:** ITD **Support:** Operations departments, SDCC, PPFD
2.3. Strengthen the work of sector and thematic and other practice groups (e.g., procurement and financial management) to expand knowledge networks—virtual and physical—to ensure that relevant knowledge is stored, shared, and communicated using the proper platforms and modalities (e.g., online communities, discussion sites, case studies).	**Lead:** SDCC, DOC **Support:** BPMSD, SPD, regional departments, OAS, PPFD
3. Strengthen and clarify measures to guide teams in developing quality knowledge products and services. Allow sufficient time to transfer tacit knowledge through learning, debriefing knowledge holders, and codifying the knowledge.	
3.1. Develop department road maps to ease the application of KMAP principles to department-specific knowledge management actions to align the KMAP to departments' business needs.	**Lead:** All departments
3.2. Contribute to ADB as a learning organization by (i) coordinating the development of sector and thematic learning programs and country knowledge exchange; and (ii) employing after-action reviews, case study discussions, peer review measures, and the findings of the Independent Evaluation Department.	**Lead:** Operations departments **Support:** All departments (SDCC for STG programs)
3.3. Review the knowledge components in technical assistance programs that advance priority knowledge work and operations, using the criteria of relevance (knowledge gaps), sustainability, dissemination, reputation risk, and partnership opportunities.	**Lead:** All departments (sector directors, country directors, STG chiefs)
3.4. Develop a clear and meaningful peer review process for internal and external knowledge products and knowledge solutions, ensuring that the right experts (internal and external) review the documents early on. Ensure that peer reviewers are recognized, leading to improved staff profiles and reputations.	**Lead:** All departments

continued on next page

Table continued

Theory of Change: Pillars and Actions to Achieve Desired Results	Responsibility
PILLAR 3: RELATIONSHIPS **1. Create a culture of collaboration through strategic and efficient knowledge partnerships, and improve the quality of relationships with the ADB Institute and with governments, academia, civil society, the private sector, and others.**	
1.1. Continuously review ADB's overall approach and current practices with respect to knowledge partnerships to identify areas for improvement. Propose how ADB can engage in, communicate with, and develop strategic knowledge collaboration workplans with the ADB Institute as ADB's think tank, and with external partners such as governments, academia, and the private sector. Produce measurable outputs and meet performance indicators.	**Lead:** Knowledge management group, SDCC-KC, SPD, DOC **Support:** All departments
2. Strengthen the resident missions' role in advancing relationships.	
2.1. Align the KMAP with the knowledge management recommendations of the review of ADB's resident mission operations, particularly on (i) "One ADB" country teams,[d] (ii) strengthening of the role of resident missions as client and program units,[e] (iii) deepening of country diagnostics, and (iv) sharpening of the country focus of knowledge operations with "resident mission service windows."	**Lead:** SPD **Support:** SDCC, operations departments, ERCD
3. Strengthen relationships between ADB functions and foster a "One ADB" approach.	
3.1. Review and reconfirm the roles of key actors (country directors and resident missions, sector directors and sector divisions, sector and thematic groups, among others) in client relationships, program and portfolio development, development of a "One ADB" approach, and the use of the new ADB client management system.	**Lead:** SPD, SDCC **Support:** All other departments
4. Where relevant and they add value, nurture relationships with international financial institutions and other intergovernmental organizations on knowledge management.	
4.1. To learn from the experiences of others in effective knowledge management, engage with and seek to formalize the community of practice on knowledge management among international financial institutions and multilateral development banks, where doing so adds value for ADB.	**Lead:** SDCC **Support:** SPD

ADBI = ADB Institute; BPMSD = Budget, People, and Management Systems Department; DMC = developing member country; ERCD = Economic Research and Regional Cooperation Department; ITD = Information Technology Department; KMAP = Knowledge Management Action Plan; PPFD = Procurement, Portfolio and Financial Management Department; SDCC = Sustainable Development and Climate Change Department; SPD = Strategy, Policy and Partnerships Department; STGs = sector and thematic groups.

[a] A guidance note on preparing dynamic country knowledge plans is being prepared.

[b] *Review of ADB's Resident Mission Operations*, Action Plan, **2.4 Sharpen country focus of knowledge operations.** (i) Reform business processes for knowledge products and services to enable more effective management by resident missions and quality control by knowledge departments. (ii) Establish a knowledge clearinghouse to better match knowledge department programs with operational needs and review and align staff instructions accordingly. (iii) Develop the country focus of the Sustainable Development and Climate Change Department and the Economic Research and Regional Cooperation Department (in addition to the country workplans under action 1.1).

[c] *Review of ADB's Resident Mission Operations*, Action Plan, **2.2 Deeper diagnostics on country engagement.** (i) Regularly assess (at least once during the country partnership strategy cycle) country sector, cross-sector, and/or private sector development (with Private Sector Operations Department support). (ii) Update sector or thematic road maps. (iii) Strengthen country economist positions to create sufficient internal capacity to coordinate country diagnostics.

[d] *Review of ADB's Resident Mission Operations*, Action Plan, **1.3 "One ADB" country teams.** (i) Define terms of reference of country teams to include maintaining ADB's cutting-edge understanding of country issues, and developing the best solutions to meet development needs, including integrated solutions. (ii) Formalize country teams widened to the Private Sector Operations Department; the Sustainable Development and Climate Change Department; the Economic Research and Regional Cooperation Department; the Procurement, Portfolio, and Financial Management Department; and the Office of Public–Private Partnership. (iii) Make team members accountable for the country team objectives. (iv) Include country team tasks in staff workplans, with country director feedback on performance. (v) Systematize country director (or delegate) performance feedback on staff members of any department directly contributing to country operations.

e *Review of ADB's Resident Mission Operations,* Action Plan, **2.1 Sharpen role of resident missions as client and program units**. (i) Confirm the country director's and/or resident mission's leading role in client relationships, sovereign program and portfolio, and development of "One ADB" approaches. (ii) Confirm the sector director's and/or the sector division's leading role in sector issues and end-to-end accountability for all sovereign operations in the sector. (iii) Strengthen the role of external relations officers in resident missions, including standardizing a direct reporting line to the country director.

Source: Asian Development Bank.

APPENDIX 6

Template for Department Knowledge Management Action Plan Road Maps

The road map needs to link with the business planning process: (i) country partnership strategy and country knowledge program process, (ii) department workplans, (iii) internal staff knowledge needs, and (iv) developing member country future development trends. The road map will be further developed in consultation with the knowledge focal points.

Date:

Department:

Knowledge focal or team:

1. Identify the purpose of knowledge work

WHAT knowledge?	{Identify focus areas relevant for the department's core business.} {Identify tacit and/or documented as well as any valuable knowledge at risk (e.g., knowledge that can be lost because few experts hold it or experts who hold it are about to retire).}	{List the relevant country partnership strategies and country knowledge plans that are under preparation; country operational business plans; new solutions, projects, and/or deals; regional cooperation and integration approaches.} {List knowledge "containers." (Where is the knowledge located—in a person, an archive, a tool, a document?)}
HOW is knowledge applied?	{Identify critical areas of policy dialogue (regional, national), and capacity development and innovation projects and/or initiatives.}	{List knowledge management tools being applied, tested.}
WHO creates, identifies, and applies knowledge?	{Identify key internal and external partners. Define the role of knowledge focals.}	{List the collaboration tools being used.}

2. Adapt the Knowledge Management Action Plan to department needs

Pillars	**Phase 1** (2021)	**Phase 2** (2022–2023)	**Phase 3** (2024–2025)
People and culture			
Processes and systems			
Relationships			

GLOSSARY

knowledge	–	information or understanding that enables action to create value through increased productivity and innovation (ADB [Strategy and Policy Department, Sustainable Development and Climate Change Department, and Department of External Relations]. 2016 Knowledge Products and Services: Definition and Reporting. Memorandum. 28 April [internal])
knowledge asset	–	accumulated information and knowledge of an organization that are relevant to its core businesses and operations
knowledge competence	–	ability to apply knowledge and skills to achieve intended results in development and delivery of knowledge services, knowledge asset management, collaboration and partnership, technical application, and change management and adoption
knowledge management governance	–	organization members' roles and responsibilities in generating and capturing information and/or knowledge and accumulating an organization's knowledge assets
knowledge management	–	process of ensuring proper generation, storage, acquisition, dissemination, and use of knowledge to meet an organization's objectives
knowledge solution	–	knowledge-based practical ideas, designs, approaches, products, and processes that resolve problems (ADB [Department of Communications; Economic Research and Regional Cooperation Department; Sustainable Development and Climate Change Department; and Strategy, Policy and Partnerships Department]. 2019. Measuring, Reporting and Recognizing Knowledge Products and Services and Knowledge Solutions. Memorandum. 19 October [internal])

| tacit knowledge | – | knowledge that is difficult to articulate or capture through writing or recording. The tacit knowledge of ADB resides in its staff, sector and thematic groups, and practice groups, and is embedded in its projects and programs |
| Theory of Change | – | a set of causal relationships that determine how a set of actions will bring about the most desired outcomes for intended beneficiaries |

www.ingramcontent.com/pod-product-compliance
Lightning Source LLC
Chambersburg PA
CBHW042011230326
41599CB00059B/7423